T0065171

The
BUSINESS
of *Living*

DORN'S OTHER BOOKS

Strands of Rhyme: Poems from the Real World
Poetry, My First Language
The Joy of Jewish Holidays in Rhyme
Monica's Chanukah & More

The
BUSINESS
of *Living*

Essays of Existence

RITA FIDLER DORN

To order additional copies of this book, contact:
Xlibris
844-714-8691
www.Xlibris.com
Orders@Xlibris.com
850096

INTRODUCTION

Hello, Dear Reader,
Welcome to my world— the world of words, reading,
and writing. <u>The Business of Living</u> is a collection of
pieces reflecting some of what has been my business,
throughout my life, as well as the business of people
whom I know. Hopefully they are universal enough
to relate to your life, as well. This book is gently
interactive. Living is, indeed, a business,
and how well we run our business determines
how successful and satisfying it is, and thus how
"profitable." Life, after expenses (loss) should show
some profit (success), so we can consider it a worthwhile
investment.
R.F.D.

DEDICATION

To my husband Jeffrey, who has been my loyal and loving partner on this colorful ride that we call Life.

IN MEMORY

Remembering, with love, my parents, Beatrice and David Fidler; my brother, Eric Stephan Fidler; and my in-laws, Joan and Frank Dorn.

TABLE OF CONTENTS

LOVE STORIES

WAR STORIES

POTPOURRI

FOOD

"Man shall not live by bread alone…:"
—*Moses (whom Jesus later quoted)*

"Life is uncertain. Eat dessert first."
—*Ernestine Ulmer, Sophisticated Gourmet.*

"Tell me what you eat, and I will tell you who you are."
—*Jean Anthelme Brillat-Savarin*

Food, An Art Form

If words are an art form (poetry) and
sound is an art form (music),
then food is surely an art form too.
We take the raw material and
cut, chop, pare, dice or slice it
to our preference.
We might add spices to alter the flavor a bit.
Then we submit it to heat
on the stove in a pot,
in a sauté pan, or in the hot, hot oven.
We arrange it artfully on plate or platter,
now having a relationship with it, and,
after our *oohs* and *ahs*,
it gets promptly consumed,
no one even remembering its name an hour later.
A shame it cannot last as long as the painting on the wall,
or a sculpture on a pedestal, or
even a photograph in a frame.
A shame. Such good art.

Tea and Coughing

Ever since I was a little girl, when I got sick, I coughed. I coughed deeply, richly, commandingly, and aggressively . . . so hard that I felt its vibrations, from my throat up to my temples and from my throat radiating down my upper arms all the way to my elbows, and often reaching my solar plexus. Sometimes I even felt it marathon all the way down my legs.

I coughed profoundly and harshly, often producing, well, you know, colored spit. Phlegm it was called. Not sure which word is more gross, *phlegm* or *spit*. Other times, I just hacked away without any product, sounding like a saw. This coughing played havoc with the skin on my throat, so that it soon became raw and tender.

After each coughing "stanza," I would sigh deeply and moan a little, weakened from the experience but wanting to verbalize it in some way. Cough syrups' effect was short-lived and I swigged it right from the bottle instead of bothering with the tablespoon's meager measure; I used it as needed, rather than by schedule.

One time, according to my personal diagnosis, I dislodged an early pregnancy with the gargantuan strength and herculean power of my coughing— so far-reaching and powerful was its influence.

Coughing, like other symptoms of illness, is usually worse at night. When I was a child, held captive in the clutches of an unfriendly cold or frequently visiting bronchitis, I would awake in the nocturnal dark: coughing, wheezing, sighing, and moaning. Always in that order.

On those occasions, my mother would get up out of her warm bed, go downstairs to the kitchen, and perform the nurturing act of making me some "tea." Now my mother was not a tea drinker and didn't like the taste; thus, we did not keep tea leaves or tea bags in the house. So what she did was pour boiling water into a waiting cup, where a generous teaspoon or two of grape jelly sat waiting. That gave the liquid brew some color as well as sweetness. She brought it upstairs to me and sat on the side of my bed as we waited together for it to cool. My coughing abated for awhile, after a cup of "tea," and I could go back to sleep.

Even now, when I think of "tea," especially when I am sick, my first vision is purple liquid in a white, bone china teacup on a matching saucer, steaming sweetly: the symbol of treatment and of my mother's devotion to me.

***Third Place winner, Pinecrest Library
Summer Essay Contest 2017***

Diet Junkie

I'm a diet junkie, a sucker for every new food plan
that hits the streets. . . or the web.
Juice fasting, fruit smoothies, veggie shakes. I'm in.
Grapefruit diet, plant based vegetarian or vegan,
fruititarian or pescatarian. Sign me up.
Broth-based soup with only green vegetables as passengers on
that train. OK, I'll cook.
Weight Watchers, Jenny Craig, Med Spa packaged foods.
Sure.
Quick Weight Loss Center with grocery food but pushing their
signature bars, shakes, supplements. Yep.
Health spas always catch my eye, from the posh to the rustic.
I go there and never fail to do well, exercise like a maniac, and
lose weight, feel euphorically content with the meager fare they
serve, swearing up and down the lamp posts that I will continue
the regimen at home until my last excess pound is shed. And
when I swear the above, I truly believe that I can and that I
will, blissfully ignoring my history—the long, caravan of
unhappy endings.
Diet junkie.
I got initiated as a preteen, when, at 15 pounds overweight,
I was threatened by my mother that if I didn't lose weight
I would never get married. I believed her, but not enough to
mend my ways. Just enough to feel shamed by my body. She

warned me that I would have to buy my clothes at Omar the Tentmaker.

As a young adult, a mature adult, and an older adult, I consistently viewed the newest diet, plan, pill, book, program, or fat farm as a panacea, the messiah, my prince charming, the one for whom I had been waiting all my life. My *beshayrt* (destiny, fate), the genie who would be the genuine and permanent game-changer. But of course, it never was. Therefore, I am still hooked, not thin yet, but not yet saying "screw you" to the fat. Still a diet junkie.

EPILOGUE: Actually, a few years ago, I decided to say "screw you" to being fat and decided to just live with it and work around it. Strangely enough, shortly thereafter, my sweet tooth and cravings disappeared, and I found myself able to make rational —not emotional— food decisions. Pretty surprised but hey, who's complaining? I am often not hungry at mealtime and so I skip it or just have a bowl of soup. On days in which I overeat carbs, the next day I easily decrease them. Pretty amazing. Who am I? Who have I become? Beats me. Not desperate to be reed thin because I know that won't happen, but I don't consider myself a diet junkie anymore.

Country Club Dining Room

An abundant or over-abundant amount of food.
Almost obscenely abundant.
Don't let a vision of abject poverty and starvation
interrupt this charming meal. Nearly endless buffet choices
on the chalk white tableclothed dais.
Aromas of cooked meat and broiled fish
waft through the spacious dining hall.
All beautifully presented,
food is well dressed in its Sunday best,
hoping to be adopted by the diners and
"taken home" with them to their tables.

If successful, they will be admired.
"What a beautiful salmon!."
"Such colorful fruit salad!"
"Farm fresh lettuce in this Cobb salad."
"This egg soufflé is so puffy!"
Following the compliments, of course, is the eating.

Hopefully, the praise will continue.
"Delicious." "Very tasty." "Mmm, seasoned just right."

Club members and guests pause
from the process of eating, for some small social chat,

to glance across the table at their comrades,
or better yet out of the expansive windows,
unblemished by small panes or dividers of any sort,
at the rolling green golf course.

A gentle wait staff person appears,
offering to bring anything that might be lacking.
"Yes, I would love a hard-boiled egg for my salad, Charles."
"Right away, Mrs. Z."
He returns promptly with a
shelled hard-boiled egg in a small silver footed cup.
Knowing the routine, he begins to remove the soft white
outside for his patron as she only wants the cooked yolk to
sprinkle on her farm fresh lettuce.
"Yes, that's fine, Charles."
"Very good, Mrs. Z." Charles disappears.
Shortly, a *sommelier* glides by to
refill the wine glasses without even being summoned.

A small woman in waitress garb and a beaming smile
appears with a wheeled cart holding a huge coffee urn
and a few dessert representatives:
Chilled Key Lime pie. Warm apple strudel.
Rich German chocolate 7-layer cake.
"There's also ice cream I could bring you," she
offers helpfully.
"Rum raisin, cherry nut, and banana cream today."
"If you want something else, I could look in the kitchen
freezer for you"
"Cherry nut sounds perfect, Gladys."
"You too, Adele,?" Mrs. Z. encourages her guest.
Adele nods in agreement.
Mrs. Z. whispers conspiratorially to Gladys, "How about a
little of that nice Grand Marnier poured over it.?" She pauses.
"Good for my sore throat," she adds with a grin.

"Of course, Mrs. Z. I'll be right back."
The two diners complete their meal
and leisurely stroll out of the dining room
toward the sunlight. The guest thanks her host for her
hospitality, which the club member shrugs off.

"It's nothing. We're accessed a monthly fee here
for this dining room, so we may as well use it.
Be charged for it, whether we do or not. But it's OK.
Nice place. Attentive staff, and we can
keep an eye on the golf course.
That always makes me feel happy."

The Purple Menace

Vegetables, vegetables, yes, I have met many vegetables and most of the family members I have liked and enjoyed being friends with. I ate them and valued our relationship. But as in any family group, there are always some whom we do not like as well their relatives. For me, this black sheep of the vegetable family would have to be the eggplant.

The first thing I do not like about the eggplant is its **name**. When I hear the name, I think of an egg—round, oval, small, and white, and of a plant—green, leafy, and growing in someone's garden. However, that is not even close to what an eggplant looks like. An eggplant is about the size of my fist, dark purple, smooth, and sort of pear shaped. I like things to look like their names, and this one does not.

The next thing that offends me about the eggplant is that its purple **skin** must be peeled off with a knife before cooking it. Purple is not a bad color, but when it is removed, the pale, sickly-looking cream-colored inside meat is revealed. This must be sliced to be cooked or chopped up to make eggplant salad.

Anyhow this eggplant has a very nasty **personality** trait. If, after the skin is removed, the cream-colored inner part isn't fried or chopped or processed very soon, it begins to turn a threatening color of brown, bit by bit. The progression continues until the menacing brown has completely conquered the white. Then, of course, it is totally impossible for me to ever consider eating it.

When I first met my husband, he was always telling me how much he liked eggplant—thinly sliced and fried in a pan like little potato pancakes or made into salad and mixed with a cold sauce. He also enjoyed it under a blanket of melted cheese, eggplant *parmesian*, or drenched in a jacket of spicy tomato sauce, eggplant *marinara*. Yuck on all counts. Now I admit that anything with cheese on it can't be all bad, but eggplant really pushes it.

The fourth quality that that assaults me about eggplant is its **texture**. After being cooked or chopped, its consistency becomes mushy. Now mushy food is wimpy and I have always considered mushy food somewhat unintelligent. Who wants to eat stupid food? So its mushiness is another characteristic that will keep eggplant from ever being my friend.

Now let's talk about the main reason most of us eat. No, not sustenance. Not nutrition. **Taste**. A food can be very unhealthy but if it catches you in the right mood or on the right occasion, it well might find its way into your mouth if it tastes good. So eggplant fails the taste test for me. I find it bitter. It is not crunchy. It is not sweet. And it is not smooth. Its taste has absolutely no redeeming qualities for my very discriminating palate.

Suppose I were a teacher and the eggplant were a student in my class. At report card time, the eggplant's grades would look something like this:

Name	D+
Skin Color	C
Personality	D-
Texture	D-
Taste	F

Thus, I guess it's safe to say that the vegetable which most offends me is the eggplant. I consider it a true menace to diners who appreciate the green, yellow, white, and orange members of the vegetable family— much finer nutritional friends on all counts.

Ice Cream Saga

When I was a child, my mom bought ice cream for the family, from the drug store. Then, as now, I loved ice cream. It's still my favorite dessert and I never want to see the bottom of the dish. Anyhow, she would buy a pint, to divide among the four of us: two parents, my brother, and me. One pint. Usually butter pecan. We ate it in low, round, clear glass dessert dishes.

Some of my friends' parents invested in ice cream soda glasses, into which they would mix ice cream, milk, seltzer or a flavored carbonated soft drink, like Coke or black cherry, which in Cleveland in the 1950's we called "pop." Those tall vessels were regal.

My mom scooped the ice cream out of the square little box with a soup spoon. Having seen real ice cream scoopers at my friends' houses, just like the ones they used at the drug store soda fountain, I asked my mom why we didn't get an ice scoop, which made perfectly round balls of ice cream. Sometimes my friends had colored sprinkles and hot fudge, but I didn't even bother asking about those. Her answer to the scooper question was familiar: "It's not necessary."

At my friends' houses, there was always a wide choice of flavors. Their parents would say, "What flavor would you like, Rita? We have chocolate marshmallow, strawberry banana, French vanilla, and, oh, here's some mint chip." Wow, so many options. Just like at the soda fountain. Furthermore, some kitchens had clear cylindrical containers filled with pastel colored straws, and when the home ice cream sodas were complete, we could each choose two of those! They also had long, skinny spoons we used. So much fun—like a party, even though it wasn't anybody's birthday.

I enjoyed the nights we had ice cream at home, as long as I didn't think about the ice cream ritual at my friends' houses. Looking back, now, I can't help wondering why my mom didn't buy a few pints in different flavors or maybe a quart or even a half-gallon! We had a freezer section at the bottom of our refrigerator. Or why she didn't get a real ice cream scoop. Could it have cost 29 cents? Even in those days, that wasn't a lot. Or the fancy soda glasses? I guess she might have defended the one pint at a time issue by saying that all those extra calories in the house weren't necessary.

Now that I'm an adult, when my husband comes home with two or three gallons of ice cream, I am tempted to say "Why so much? Why so many?" but I stifle the words. We don't have ice cream soda glasses, but we do have a real metal scooper and frequently pour *creme de menthe* or chocolate cordial over the top of our ice cream. I still love the taste of ice cream and still never want to reach the bottom of the dish.

How do you remember childhood ice cream?
What was your favorite flavor then? Now?

TIME

"Time and tide wait for no man."

*--Geoffrey Chaucer's Prologue to the
Clerk's Tale, about 1395*

"The bad news is time flies. The good news is that you're the pilot."

—*Michael Altshuler*

"Time is precious. Make sure you spend it with the right people."

—*Anonymous*

"All things fear Time, but time fears the Pyramids."

—*Herodotos, ancient Greek historian and geographer*

"How we spend our days is, of course, how we spend our lives."

—*Annie Dillard*

A Face from The Past

Palm Springs Junior High School, Hialeah, Florida
September 1964. 7th grade English class.

Askew? *Here*. Carpenter? *Here*. Critcher? *Here*. Esfakus? Here.
Love? *Here*. Lowy? *Here*. McIlhenny? *Here*. Nabatovsky? Here.
Orlando? *Here*. Renderer? *Here*. Romero? *Here*. Rosendorn? Here.
Trujillo? *Here*.

The first year teacher, Miss Fidler, was taking attendance and the students were settling in, still tan from summer beaches and fidgety from the unwelcome end of their sunny vacations. The school had many newly arrived Cuban children with a lot of adjusting to do—language, culture, friends, behaviors, expectations. The first year of anything is often memorable and this one was too.

Miss Fidler thought she was going to save the world by teaching her beloved English that she hoped they would appreciate: grammar (so easy, for her); literature (to expand their views of life and people); essay writing (during which she played classical music); spelling contests, poetry, book reports, posters, reading a textbook play aloud outdoors on a beautiful morning with the whole class sitting under a big tree (for which she almost got fired because she hadn't checked leaving the classroom with the principal who kept a tight rein on everyone — students and staff alike.)

The students learned some of what she taught, liked some of it, and disliked some of it. They thought Miss Fidler was a good teacher, but too strict. She always insisted that they keep quiet when she or others were speaking. The kids loved her projects and group activities. One of their assignments was to decorate the small showcase in the hallway next to their classroom door with artifacts related to material they were learning about. It won a school prize that year.

The boy whose name was Romero was a slim, good looking guy who was a Romeo with the girls. The Askew kid suffered from a lot of peer teasing. Trujillo had a heavy Spanish accent but lots of enthusiasm and a big smile. Nabatovsky said she wanted to be a nurse some day. Lowy was thoughtful, respectful, and a very good student who got all A's. He had black wavy hair and a serious manner. He seemed at peace with himself and confident, but not egotistic.

Anyway, that year ended and the 7th graders moved on to 8th, 9th, 10th grades and the rest of their lives. Miss Fidler taught there for 2 more years and switched to Carol City Senior High because she preferred the upper grades and also because that newer school had air conditioning. She, too, progressed into the rest of her life, taught in several high schools, went back and got a masters degree so she could teach on the college level, and eventually semi-retired.

Here she was in the Digital Age, complete with all the goodies it offered, like Facebook. Miss Fidler, now Mrs. Dorn, noticed on Facebook a name which seemed familiar, from her first year of teaching. Louis Lowy. He was friends with some of her poetry colleagues. Could it be the same person? Now grown up, of course. She FB messaged him and—good grief—it was! He said that he remembered her and that she had influenced him in that 7th grade English class those long years ago. She recalled that he did all his homework, was well-behaved, and caused no problems in her classroom. He was very reserved, with much poise for a 7th grader. She always thought he would become a success. She was delighted to learn he felt she had made an impression on him.

That once 13-year old boy was now married, had two college-aged children of his own, was a musician, a retired fire fighter, and a published novelist! How could this all happen? Furthermore, Louis Lowy was a member of South Florida Writers Association, to which Ricki Dorn belonged, although he admitted he did not attend meetings frequently. They chatted on Facebook and finally met up in person, first at a library poetry reading and later at SFWA meetings. To one meeting, he brought a folder to show her, which contained a report he had written for her class; he said he found it among some old papers in his house. In her writing was her comment on it, "Very good" with the grade of A-.

Small world? Yes, but so interesting how faces of our past often follow us into our future or show up after being "absent" for a long time.

April in Atlanta

When 6,000 composition teachers convened at the Marriott Marquis Hotel in Atlanta, Georgia, from April 7-9, 2011 for the annual College Composition and Communications Conference, (fondly called 4C) I was fortunate enough to be one of them. With a small grant from FIU where I teach and the encouragement of my husband, I left Miami on American Airlines before 7 am on Thursday, feeling expectant and excited. I was not disappointed. Current regulations now require airport arrivals of 90-120 minutes before take-off of domestic flights. Due to a surprisingly uncrowded MIA and an atypically efficient agent, I completed my check-in in five minutes and had an hour and 55 minutes left; not even the shops were open yet. After a pretty good egg on an English muffin and a coffee from Nathan's, (shades of Coney Island recalled) I walked to the gate and settled in for some serious people watching of the few very sleeping-looking other passengers. I had a couple of books with me, but was too wired to read.

Just to give you some background: professors present papers, offer workshops, and conduct presentations on every imaginable topic related to the

composition classroom. The global conference theme
was "Immigration in the Classroom;" therefore, the
session topics addressed diversity of every possible
kind of student—preparedness level, gender, sexual
orientation, religion, race, fluency, giftedness, and
academic deficits.

For example, one presenter discussed the differences
in classroom behavior and attitude between the
typical college sorority girls and young women of the
same age who are incarcerated. The co-eds tried very hard to please
the professors and impress the other students, especially the guys; the
young female inmates displayed a strong "I couldn't care less" attitude.
This presenter learned this
information from a composition class that a colleague
had brought to one of the prisons in Texas. Another
talked about emotional harm done to African-
American males who are forbidden to write
compositions in "Black English." Instead of banning
the speech of these students, instructors were
encouraged to assign them to write one essay in their
cultural language, thereby giving their heritage a
respected place in the classroom.

My plane arrived in spring-like, dogwood festooned
Atlanta promptly at 8:30 and I opted for
the 10-minute $35 cab ride instead of
the $6.00 bus ride (transport time unknown).
Once in the cab, however, I noticed a sign that
offered a 20% discount to senior citizens. When
I asked the driver if that was still in effect, he said
yes but that I would have to show him my ID, proving my age.
Flattered, I willingly did so and got a 20% discount
on the cab trip to the hotel.

I was not giving a presentation, but had offered
to chair a session. I had worn jeans to travel in but
planned to change into a professional looking suit
before our session. Despite my request for early
check-in, my room was not ready. The desk clerk,
however, offered me the use of the locker room in
the spa. Not ideal, but I managed, and was ready, properly
clad, in time to attend one session before ours. That
session took place in a 500-seat ballroom with
handouts, PowerPoint, videographer, the works.
Sol Dobrin, this "famous" speaker (whom
everyone except me seemed to know), director
of writing programs at the University of Florida,
addressed the future of writing studies.

Our session met in a cozier 35-seat salon. No
cameras, media personnel, or other fanfare- just
the three very young presenters and myself. The
crowd was relaxed, attentive, friendly, and
responsive. To give you an idea of the types of
materials presented, the three papers in my
session were these:
"Tracing the Rhetorical Marker 'Illegal' and
its Role in the Deaths of Thousands of 'Illegal'
Immigrants,"
"Troubling Citizenship: Contesting Civic
Engagement in an Era of Immigration Crises,"
"Inventing Guatemala: A Feminist View of
the Ethics of Writing."
Pretty heavy-duty stuff, but also current,
relevant, and surprisingly interesting. My job was
to introduce each speaker, give a brief
précis of his or her content, conclude with an
even briefer mini-summary, and invite Q and A from
the audience. I did, they did, and it was fine.

The buzz words were "rhet-comp" and "comp-rhet" (from rhetoric and composition). The mood of presenters and audience was positive and friendly, but mostly it was involved. Everyone, at every level, was engaged. No one was negative, indifferent, or bored. Everybody seemed to care about writing, about serving students better, about dealing with composition classroom challenges, and about contributing to the future of teaching writing. It would be hard not to be sucked into the tunnel of what was going on.

My biggest frustration was choosing a session; in any given time frame, I had to select from at least 10-12 different subjects. Of course I wanted to hear them all. People entered and exited sessions at will. I walked out of only one session. The topic was tantalizing, "Defining and Teaching About the World Through World Literature." However, the reality was a panel of underprepared, timid, soft-speaking minimally-fluent students from seven different countries, not really integrating the literature of their nations into their methods of teaching composition. Disappointing.

However, the replacement session was a vibrant workshop about "Research on Student Learning," which delved into writing about writing, surface errors, visual thinking, and conceptual mapping. An audio tape accompanied the video that displayed each idea as the student said it. Three different ones were shown, illustrating students' totally different processes and paths of thought. Most presenters offered cards and email addresses for anyone who wanted more info. or the ability to keep in touch. Everyone was accessible.

The list below shows you a fraction of the vast
range of topics available:

- Staffing a Writing Center (I am involved in the
writing center at Miami Dade College)
- Blurring the Disciplinary Boundaries (bringing
people from disciplines other than English in to
teach composition classes, to present a more varied
approach. For example, an international relations
graduate said she viewed writing as merely a tool
with which to communicate ideas, while her English
major fiancé saw writing as a finished product and
a work of art... me, too)
- *Mamzers*, Our Jewish Past as a Professional Prologue
(memoirs of Jewish professors and how their
cultural background contributes to their
professional personae)
- Everybody Eats: Connecting Students to the
Discourse of Food (food for [critical] thought; food
as muse; the presenter was a food-critic turned
composition instructor)
- Modern Approaches to Teaching Grammar, Usage,
and Punctuation (self-explanatory)
- Think Tank (a forum of guidance for people who
want to present papers next year)
- Prison Writing (works of incarcerated men and
women of all ages and walks of life)
- Late-Life Writers (Alzheimers victims, nursing
homes residents, and hospice patients).

And how could I leave such a conference without
some delicious tastes of poetry? I attended a
session which discussed, analyzed, and gave
histories of the vast assortment of forms, styles,
and boundaries of poetry. That was fine, but the

best was a poetry workshop, to which we brought
not only samples of poetry to read to the others,
but copies on which they could respond and
critique. I chose my poem called "The Givens" for
this workshop; it's about what we thought were "it goes-
without-saying" expectations that we have for
our marriages, our spouses, and our children and
how those expectations often are not met. When I
finished reading it, one young teacher, from Massachusetts,
said, with tears in her eyes, "I know that my mother wrote
that poem with you." We try to touch our listeners
and readers with our poetry, and sometimes we do.

To say that my presence at this conference was
energizing, informative, stimulating, moving,
illuminating, and fun is an understatement. I took
copious notes, filed the business cards, and
catalogued the handouts. I wish that each of you
could have shared it all with me. It was just grand!
Thank you for letting me give you a peek into 4C.

EPILOGUE: (for Bailey Smith Barash):
When the conference concluded, my sister-in-law, Dr. Pamela Dorn
Sezgin, anthropology professor and Marietta resident, picked me up and
we took a drive-by tour of the spots on Peachtree Street which had been
my hangouts in the early 70's, when I was single and then dating my
future husband. We passed the High Art Museum where I had enjoyed
many fine exhibits and The Academy Theatre where I had taken some
drama classes and seen fresh, original, alternative plays. We stopped
in for a bite at Gene and Gabe's, an Italian restaurant, still staffed by
friendly gay waiters and whose walls were decorated with huge real oil
paintings (maybe not famous oils but real ones anyhow). I waved at the
spot where the Iron Horse Greek Restaurant had been, now supporting
a dry cleaner; the Iron Horse was where my husband Jeff took me on

our very first date, August 14, 1969. The Temple, where I had taught Sunday School, was also on our agenda.

The high point of our afternoon was a visit back to the Darlington Apartments, a 6-story brick building with an ever-changing population sign in front, where I lived for about a year before marrying and moving in with Jeffrey. I became good friends with another young single girl, Bailey Smith, recently returned from biology graduate studies in Australia. I lived on the 6th floor and she on the 5th floor, both of us inhabiting identical exiguous studio apartments. We shared experiences and confidences; she attended my wedding the following July, outdoors, in waterfalled Winn Park.

I told Pamela how I recalled the spacious lobby which then had housed a small grocery shop, package store, hair salon, and luncheonette where I often ate a solitary but hot dinner. As we parked and then entered the front door, we saw in the stark, bare lobby, only two large metal desks and two uniformed security guards. No shops of any kind. "Oh my God," I thought, "We will never be able to get upstairs." However, I pleaded my case to the guards, anyhow, telling them how I was back in Atlanta for a visit and wanted to see at least the door to the apartment where I had lived more than 30 years earlier as a young woman. To our surprise, one of them smiled and said "Sure, go on up. Elevators are over there!" Good thing he said that because they were in a different location from their earlier one.

Pam and I found our way into the 6th floor hall from the elevator and walked a few units down the corridor to what I thought had been my home, now not entirely certain of the number. As we stood there, deliberating as to whether we should knock on the door, it opened and a young Indian woman, apparently leaving to go someplace, appeared. She looked surprised to see us, of course, and we explained our presence. "Sure," she said cordially, "Come on in and welcome home!"

Wow, pretty trusting of her, I thought. We entered and looked around the now seemingly very small unit, nearly devoid of any furniture, save a few sleeping pallets on the floor. "We are getting reading to move," she explained, "and most of our furniture has already gone to the next place." Somehow I doubted that there had ever been any more furniture there, but we exchanged a few pleasantries. I recalled the two singles (beds by night and couches by day), my stuffed bookcase, a desk of course, a dresser in the miniscule dressing room, and a table with two chairs in a dining corner to eat on whatever I had cooked in the tiny galley of a kitchen. It was small but had been operative. It did not seem that little when I lived there; in fact, I had felt it was almost roomy. I also recalled Bailey's identical studio on the floor below me, which sported batik fabric covered pillows, interesting little figurines from across the world, and tea—lots of tea, which she brewed for us often.

We bid the kind lady goodbye, thanked her for letting us in to reminisce, and proceeded to my sister-in-law's large, well-furnished home in the Marietta suburbs, to rest and get ready for dinner out later that evening with Pamela and her husband, Mesut.

So, I guess the famous phrase, *"You can't go home again" is not necessarily true, because I surely did.

*Title of a novel by Thomas Wolfe, 20th century author, and published posthumously in 1940.

New Year's Eve

Why do we make such a production out of New Year's Eve,
long one of the top social, hallmark events of the year?
Do we give any thought to the reasons for the hoop-la
we attach to it?

The laughter, festivities, food, and often excessive drink,
maybe DUI's, fancy clothes, group gatherings—casual or
extravagant? Why do we do this or feel we should?

Noisemakers derive from old myths that noise scares away the
Devil and evil spirits. What are we celebrating this night and
what true cause have we to do so?

The new year is not a personal accomplishment—
it is merely the passing of time.
It will arrive. . . whether or not we toast it and
whether or not we are here to see it.
What does New Year's Eve signify? The way I see it, it
simply means we are another year older.

If we are teenagers, that aging is considered a plus—
nearing a driver's license, legal drinking age, college, marriage,
career, homeownership, and family. OK.

<u>If we are mature,</u> it measures our progress, the amount of success we are accruing in life; money; what lies ahead — a new job, relationship, or house; travel; kids growing up; our contributions to the world.

<u>But if we are old</u> (you may say senior, aged, or wise if you wish, but they are all the same), that new year represents another 12-month period, moving us closer to death and to the expiration of our birth certificates. If we are elderly (another synonym) and healthy, we know that our robust days are numbered, that illness and death will catch up to us eventually. New Year's Eve marks propelling us closer to the end.

You don't like this negative outlook, Pollyanna? Ok, let's answer it another way. Let's say we are celebrating our survival of another year; we finished it without dying and are still alive and kicking enough to party hearty. Better? Sure. Take your choice of the perspective you prefer, or can bear, but we both know which one is for real. Happy New Year, all!

Quality Time

We took a class together one summer because Son said, "Mom, all we ever do together is eat. Let's do something else for our quality time." Corey had recently moved into his own apartment, and we were trying to preserve our connection with some "quality time" at least once a week. Sometimes it was Sunday morning brunch at our house or we all, with Dad, picked up healthy food and took it to the dog park, to eat at picnic tables, while our Russell terrier socialized with her "friends." Or else it was Chinese dinner, at a neighborhood restaurant.

A local church was offering a yoga class once a week and so we signed up. The group consisted of numerous chubby, middle-aged women like me, a few elderly, fragile looking men, and my 26-year old weightlifting, bike racing, healthy food eating son. The teacher was a young woman of about 30, of Indian descent but a long time resident in the states. Pretty, serene, and fit, she was a graduate student at Columbia University in the winter but spent summers in Miami (Huh? most people flee Miami's oven hot summers if they have anyplace else to go).

It was easy to see G's devotion to and deep love of yoga, teaching it and doing it, as she introduced herself and the course. She promised a wonderful vegan dinner for all of us, as a reward, when we completed her six sessions, as well as a chance to meet a real holy man, a yogi friend of hers. She said yoga offered us a respite from the stress of our daily lives and a chance to be in touch with inner selves. "Inner selves," I liked that.

Anyhow, she began slowly and I, somewhat out of shape, struggled to keep up but did not despair. I was happy to be sharing quality time with my son. Like a committed instructor, G. demonstrated the poses for the group and then came to each of us, straightening a back for better stretch or moving an arm slightly for more balance. When she came to my fairly athletic son, she said admiringly, "Oh, you are so supple. Very, very supple." She had no corrections which would have justified her touching him, nor did she invent any, so she moved on to the next pupil, seemingly sad to be leaving this apparent feast for her eyes.

She returned to the front and illustrated another pose. Soon she made her rounds again, adjusting wayward body parts as she did before. Once again, she simply stood behind my son admiring his nice body and again she deemed him," Supple, oh, soooo supple." She proceeded to the next person and by this time Son and I were struggling to suppress our giggles. By now she was in front again, showing us a much more difficult pose. We moved into that pose, son more easily than I, but my effort was respectable. And again, G. began to circulate. As she neared us, both son and I stage whispered to each other. "Supple, soooo supple." She happened to be looking at us and apparently saw and heard our commentary. Appearing to take offense, she looked very angry and skipped her critique of both of us that time. Maybe we had executed the pose so perfectly that we needed no correction or maybe she was embarrassed? By the time she reached her spot in the front once more, Son and I had recovered and were really into maintaining our now more challenging poses.

Son and I put serious expressions on our faces and concentrated because we did not want to be on bad terms with our teacher, at least not so early in the game. Eventually, she returned to our area and after absentmindedly moving my neck to a severely less comfortable position, she critiqued my son in a cool, professional voice, "Very nice," she said briskly and moved on. Very nice? What happened to "Supple. Sooooo supple"? The remaining sessions passed without incident, mother and

Son looking forward to the meditative hour we shared each week. G. was a skilled instructor and we class members improved our stances.

We all completed the course and true to her word, G. invited us to enjoy a vegan dinner. Hosted by a friend of hers, it featured a rich, organic vegetable soup, pale rice crackers, natural fruits, and herbal teas. It tasted better than it sounds. And there was a real yogi present, emanating serenity and utter peace with the world and himself. Pleasant and smiling, he circulated slowly among us, offering to schedule individual sessions with those who desired it, for a fee of course, at which he would assign them their own personal mantras. My son sprang for the 1:1 session but wouldn't tell me his mantra. We had found G's course relaxing, benefited from the stress-free hours, and loved the vegan meal. But mostly, we remembered "Supple, sooo supple."

Signs of Our Time

What would our parents and/or grandparents have thought of all this? Don't even go there.

Our friend, a plastic surgeon, helped his son and son's girlfriend welcome their new baby, having the grace not to hassle them about when or if they planned on getting married

A psychologist whom we know has, with huge effort, put aside her initial devastation that her grandson will not be baptized, because his mom (her daughter) no longer subscribes to their Catholic family faith.

Two Jewish parents, thrilled at the arrival of their first grandchild, steeled themselves to face the absence of a traditional, joyous *bris* (circumcision ceremony). *Oy.*

Two friends of ours warmly embraced the four children of their son and his girlfriend, accepting their 10-year "engagement" and not pressuring anyone for a wedding date.

Another couple welcomed their son's husband-to-be and made a lovely religious wedding for them, as requested. Also, they created rich, healthy relationships with the three siblings whom son and son-in-law adopted.

Two parents, hearing of their son's wedding plans, were shocked that the officiant would be a close friend of the couple, deputized with a 1-day secular marriage certificate— not a rabbi, priest, minister, or even a judge.

A couple with twin sons, one gay and one straight, hosted an elegant, formal wedding in their spacious backyard for the gay one and his fiancé. "We wanted to give them a gorgeous event, as we did for his brother," but this one was in the seclusion of their home, not in church or at a hall (i.e. not out in public).

A single mom embraced her unmarried daughter and new baby— housing, feeding, supporting them until daughter finished her education and could stand alone. Later, daughter asked her mom "Why didn't you tell me he (the baby daddy) was no good?" Mom answered, "You wouldn't have believed me, and I didn't want to alienate you."

Two other parents, after coping alone for years before any community support was available, are now able to refer smoothly in social conversation to "our two daughters," one of whom had been born a boy.

An elderly Jewish woman, on a visit to the out-of-state home of her son, who was married to a Catholic woman, was amazed on one of their frequent visits to the wife's church, to see her son go up to take communion. Back at his seat, he told his mother, "I converted."

One mature woman we know happily shared that the surrogate of her son and daughter-in-law was pregnant with twin girls.

The parents of a bright, social, well-adjusted college student struggled with her sexual attraction to males and females.

Our longtime family friend married a much older man and they proudly display photos of their blended family of children, children-in-law, and grandchildren, clearly showing two members of a different race.

Religious options, tradition and lack of, homosexuality, bisexuality, gay marriage, gay parenting, transgenderism, surrogacy, racial blends, wedding and relationship alternatives: signs of the present and, for sure, of the future.

These cameos are lifted from the lives of some conventional relatives, friends, and acquaintances, in Miami, in recent years.

We may be conventional but have no guarantee that our children will be. Diversity is the destination of the future, and the journey is well underway! We had all better be on board.

They Just Get Different

I. Some things get better and some things get worse but nothing stays the same. Some things don't get better or worse, but still don't stay the same; they just get different.

Whether we deem them better or worse has a lot to do with our expectations; from time to time, we should examine our expectations to see if they are current or outdated.

Even though we are adult children now it's easy to inherit our parents' values—let them keep hanging around, like old photos, Dad's tools, Mom's cookbooks or Grandma Sarah's pearls. We don't use them but haven't gotten around to relocating or replacing them.

II. My mother kept every letter and greeting card she ever received from family—husband, children, grandchildren. I inherited them and for more years than I care to admit they lived in many cartons in my garage, groups of them neatly bound up in dusty, red satin ribbons.

Finally being ready to get rid of them, I could not bring myself to just dump them in the garbage pail like rotten orange peels or week old salad, So I called some nursing homes and senior centers offering them for use in Arts and Crafts classes. The first batches were accepted gratefully, but there were more cards left and too few senior centers.

At some point I had to sit down and extract the most very special ones (like my dad's letter asking my mom to marry him and her letter accepting). I tried to be strict with myself, saying "I will not keep more than what will fit into one shoe box." I told myself these cards led long successful lives and now had outlived their purpose. I had honored their memory, and my mother's, by letting them reside in my garage, lo, these many years.

Well, I exceeded the one shoebox limit by another whole shoebox. Two boxes? Not so bad. Those were gently placed on a garage book shelf, and the others were, as I took a deep breath, squeezed my eyes shut, and uttered a brief prayer, dumped them into a big, black, shiny plastic garbage bag. I tied the tie, told myself they were going to Greeting Card Heaven, and carried them outside.

III. So why so much about greeting cards? Values, habits, rituals are all much the same. They imbed themselves in our lives, on our agenda. We and they soon think they are permanent residents. But like cars which need a check-up every 10,000 miles, so do our procedures and values. We need to be sure our values are consistent with our lives today, not the ones 10 years ago. Dell and Apple try to make sure we update our computers and cel phones. GM, Honda, and Cadillac try their best to drive their newest models into our garages. So must we check our value systems to make sure they match the world in which we live and our modern lifestyles.

IV. <u>Here is the real impetus for this saga</u>: Recently, I said to my husband of 49 years, "It's Saturday night and we have no plans. I like to go out on Saturday night." We are in our 70's, had a busy week filled with social, medical, and community events, already enjoyed lunch with some dear friends who can no longer navigate the expressway, so we had to drive to a restaurant in Pompano to see them.

My husband said in an exaggeratedly innocent tone, "Do you mean a Saturday night date with a corsage to go to a dance, or a drive-in hamburger joint followed by a drive in movie and then "parking" in your parents' driveway for an hour?"

I laughed and said, "No, just maybe dinner out or something." He answered, "Take your expectations out of your 17-year old head. We ran around all week, were already out today, and I'm tired; I did not even get my nap. You always say it doesn't matter but you still consider Saturday evening Date Night, don't you?" Well, I admitted I was tired too, and maybe didn't need to go out to dinner. We ordered in a pizza.

But why was I "antsy" as Saturday night loomed closer? Answer: Outdated, antiquated values. My husband is retired, I still have a satisfying career, and we are grandparents. So why was my 17-year old value still poking its head up and calling me? Because I had not officially and consciously retired that value.

Some things don't get better or worse, but still don't stay the same——they just get different.

The Anatomy of Time

Time is a strange commodity. We use it, anticipate it, remember it. We can rent it but not own it. We organize it and schedule it. We think it belongs to us, and get very possessive about it; in reality, it is not ours at all—never was and never will be.

Then, why do we get offended about losing it or wasting it, obsessive about saving it? Saving it for what? For a rainy day?
Unlike money, we cannot bank it or put it under the mattress.
We cannot trade it with others, like boys did years ago with baseball cards. We cannot turn it into something else or transfer it.

Yet, so often, when we reminisce, we fondly refer to a particular era in our lives. We ask, "Where did those years go?"
They did not go anywhere.
They just evaporated, after being consumed.
Time always disappears eventually, whether or not we "use" it.
People advise others to use it wisely.
Does that mean cleverly rather than stupidly?
Frugally rather than extravagantly.
Perhaps extravagantly is better use of it, if enjoyed.

Maturely rather than childishly?
Precisely what are wise and foolish uses of time? Hard to say.

Perhaps "good" uses of time are those which, upon reflection,
we view as having been satisfactory or fulfilling; happy ones.

So how should we view our personal relationship with time?
Friendly? Flexible? Not controlling. Not intimate We shouldn't get too
cozy with it because it will eventually abandon us. Reciprocal? Hardly.
We do not pay for it nor does it respond. It's truly a one-way street. Time
is available to all of us, as long as we are alive. It's free but has a deadline.

What we do mostly with time is divide it up, section it out, assign those
sections names: minutes, hours, days, months, years, holidays. That's
when we believe we can control it, when we put labels on it: work, party,
study, cook, run, read, sing, eat, dance, sleep. dentist appointment,
board meeting, lunch date, football game, class. The list goes on. We
convince ourselves that it belongs to us. But if it doesn't, to whom does
it belong? To all of us, but none of us.

It's like a one night stand, urgent in the moment, but we'd best not ask
or anticipate anything more. If we do, we will be abandoned, hurt, and
disappointed. Dumped.

Funny how we have so much of it, but no power over it and
no expectation of having true control over it—
especially considering how intimate we are with it and
how much we talk about it, think about it, and look at it.
But, to tell the truth, genuine intimacy with time is not possible. Sounds
like a bad investment with which to become involved, but, of course,
we cannot escape it either. Weird, isn't it?

Hands

The hands of time
show lines of the years,
some for recent sorrow and
some for ancient tears.

Wrinkles and crevices
meet at junctions of skin.
These are relationships and
implications within.

The islands of smooth
speak of peace and times serene,
when neither pain nor darkness
would dare to intervene.

Purple veins and sun spots
are colors of joy and smiles,
recalling happy moments
traveled over thousands of miles.

A baby's small hands are puffy and smooth;
to work they are yet unknown;
soon they'll grow and mature,
becoming the hands of age, no more alone.

The hands of time
are the owner's life tales:
chants of buoyant joy and
trembling, morose wails.

Look now at <u>your</u> hands.
What do they tell? what do you see?
What do they promise and
where will they lead you, eventually?

WEATHER
& NATURE

"Wherever you go, always bring your own sunshine."

–Anthony D'Angelo

"Weather forecast for tonight: Dark."

— George Carlin

"Who has seen the wind?
Neither you nor I,
but when the trees bow down their heads,
the wind is passing by."

—Christina Rossetti

One Family's Trial with One 'Cane

Part I: PRE
standing in long lines at the grocery store
chatting with a neighbor, feeling connected
playing hide and seek with giant jugs of water and
        mega-sized packages of batteries
stocking up on cans of tuna and boxes of snack bars
wondering when the power will fail and for how long
bearing the albatross of no computer and no TV.
putting up hurricane shutters and letting the kids help
checking to see which stores are still open
keeping an eye on evacuation orders
locating hurricane shelters, just in case
finding the Scrabble set
checking in with friends and family
filling up the gas tank, more long lines
"hurricane"— the word takes on a new meaning,
        abandoning the University of Miami team

Part II: DURING

surveying all of the windows
letting the children stay up late
making popcorn while the microwave still works
identifying the guerrilla-like sounds outside the battened-down
        house: city windies, whip drips, rain slosh, crash-smash,
        bang-chang, thud-mud, trickle-thump . . . all of them
        very wet
listening for the lull that is the eye of the storm
going outside to see it, or resisting the urge to do so
telling the kids tales of past hurricanes we've weathered
finally falling asleep, only to wake up soon after, tingling
        with excitement, anxiety, concern, expectation——most
        definitely "in the moment."

Part III: POST

surveying the homestead damages
comparing our hurricane imprints to those of other houses
        on the street
keeping the children's trauma at bay
sopping up rain-soaked floors and carpets
planning to replace broken windows
putting in a call to repair guys and construction crews
lifting big wind-pummeled branches from lawn and driveway
cooking some casseroles to take to those whose kitchens
        were destroyed
phoning far away relatives to assure them that we are OK
guesstimating how much the insurance will cough up
deciding when to return to work, delaying it as long
        as possible
using up the remaining food or ordering in pizza
hoping to put the hurricane behind us—not yet, but soon.

Anything familiar here for you?
Check the ones you recall and add your own.

Hurricane Andrew Revisited

It was August 1992 and Hurricane Andrew was on his way to South Florida. We had invited my parents to leave their North Miami Beach home and stay with us in Kendall to be safe and weather the storm together with the family.

With tepid enthusiasm, they agreed and arrived with a few days' worth of clothing and, of course, a plentitude (enough for a small army) of food for our fridge, which reminded me that hurricanes are often accompanied by loss of electrical power.

Another point here is that my dad was then…I could say dying of cancer or I could say undergoing chemotherapy; either way, he was not at his strongest or in his most comfortable condition. Although we assigned them the sleeper sofa in the living room, my dad often grew weary in the daytime and so he napped in our king size bed. Now I look back and wonder why we did not give them our bedroom. It would have certainly been an act of kindness, which for some reason we didn't extend.

So now our house had 9 inhabitants: 2 grandparents, 2 parents, 2 teenaged sons, and 3 small dogs. We were full. My mother alternated between worrying about how their house would survive the storm and declaring that it was not really necessary for them to be here.

The boys were happy to have Grandma Bea and Grandpa David on the premises, and my husband, Jeff, with intermittent help from our sons, concerned himself with hurricane preparedness—stockpiling water and batteries, bringing in patio furniture, and putting up storm shutters. I kept an eye on my dad, chatted with my mom, and planned the meals for all of us, trying to use up the more perishable items first.

We kept storm vigil at radio and TV and repeatedly discussed the updates with each other. Hurricane Andrew arrived, devastating Homestead, and doing fragmented but only moderate damage to Kendall. On our street, our neighbors' trees survived the battering winds and rain, remaining upright, but the majestic ones in our front yard were all pummeled right into our driveway... across our two vehicles and my parents' car, thoroughly smashing their windshield. Now my mother had plenty to say about how they should have stayed home, reflecting that they and their car would have been perfectly safe there.

A few days later, following a visit from amiable neighbors who helped my husband and sons lift the trees from our driveway, my mom drove back to North Miami Beach with, at my persistent urging, some of the remaining food. My dad was tucked comfortably across the back seat, stretched out amidst quilt and pillows. She drove very carefully, painfully conscious of her windshield-less state. I worried about that too, but, fortunately they made the 45 minute drive home, safely. We recovered, and Hurricane Andrew took his place in history and in our memories, and we all moved forward with our lives.

Let it Snow

When I hear northerners complain about winter's cold I think fondly of how much I loved the snow of Ohio where I grew up. Snowmen and snowwomen, snow forts, snowball fights, stashing a few snowballs in the freezer for future use. Even winter clothes were loved by me: corduroy slacks, cashmere sweaters, tweed jackets, wool winter coats and vivid puffy parkas with color coordinated mittens and scarfs. At college, some of the students wore woolen nose warmers which had yarn strings tying them around the back of the head. Funny looking bur useful.

I must admit that my love for snow took place when I was a child and teenager. In my now elderly years, were I living in a snowy city, my arthritis and old bones might not like it so much.

Teenaged boys came around with big shovels offering to clear our driveway of snow so we could get the cars out and go to school, work, parties. My mom usually hired them, grateful for their service. I recall her scraping the icy snow off the front window of the car with a little gadget made of metal and a rubber strip.

When I was very young, maybe six, my dad offered to create a snowman for the me and the other little kids in our apartment building. I did not know he knew how to do that so I was very interested to see what would happen. When we all met in the back courtyard on the appointed

Saturday morning, we were disappointed to see that not much snow had fallen during the night. "Don't worry," my dad assured us.

First, he commandeered a big, clean metal garbage can and turned it upside down. Someone had left several small plastic pails out there, like the ones kids use in the sandbox in summer. Then, he distributed the pails among us and told us to gather with our mittened hands as much snow as we could put into the pails and bring them to him. Meantime, he found a few large stones and a curved twig branch. We brought him our pails of snow, the contents of which he poured onto what was the bottom of the metal garbage can, now at the top, making a nice, thick, white cushion. We helped him place the stones where eyes and nose belonged, and he used the twig to make a thin but smiling mouth.

One kid took off his red knit hat and gave it to our snowman. My dad told us that the snowman needed a name and another kid said, "Let's call him Mr. Fluffy," and so we gleefully did. Thus, despite a meager amount of snow that morning, we got our snowman and my dad was a hero.

The wooden sled with steel gliders that my brother and I shared was a precious winter toy on which we used to take turns pulling each other, when snow covered our neighborhood sidewalks. I always enjoyed the snow of my childhood and miss it even now. "Let it snow, let it snow, let it snow" was my mantra. These days, watching winter news on TV, I look fondly at the snow, even the storms of it.

Your feelings, memories, attitudes about snow?

The Life of a Fire

We decided to eat dinner in the backyard last night, at our round, iron, patio table near the chiminea— a recent find and delightful new resident in our personal jungle.

After generously stocking the chiminea with birch logs, we brought the pistol lighter close. the flames exploded, wildly asserting their presence, like a newborn baby squalling to herald its entrance into the world. the flames flailed their arms about, peaks skimming the restricting walls of the ceramic jailer, not unlike the slats of a crib, limiting the extended energetic limbs of a baby.

The flames made their rounds, moving from log to log,
leaving a souvenir on each one, growing taller and wider every moment; soon all the logs were ablaze with the golden contagion of the fire. it whipped back and forth, from left to right, visiting ceiling, walls, and wooden "floor."

Announcing its undeniable control, the fire matured,
constantly growing bolder and bigger and more productive—taking captive the kindling, and hotly influencing every inch of the chiminea's interior walls. it never stopped moving, even for a second. its dancing gyrations attracted our attention, mesmerizing us.

After some time, almost imperceptibly, it began to diminish, slowly losing strength and speed, gradually decreasing the span of its territory, and occasionally rallying for a temporary comeback, resisting its imminent demise.

The limber flames no longer grouped themselves with friends
and colleagues, but now limped, in pairs or as singles;
few flames survived, as some of their number expired,
leaving the stalwarts to their loneliness..... still moving but
submissively now.

The timber, originally fat, robust, healthy logs—
a scenic canvas stage for the active flames—
had become skinny, almost skeletal, the shorter rectangles suggesting
coffins on which a few flames now gently tip-toed as the flickers
disappeared, the silhouette of the remaining wooden landscape,
irregular and randomly chunky,
recalled a ghost town, whose residents had left or died.

Logs in the back had taken the shape of thin trees,
their spiky branches reaching out blindly to whoever might pass,
but no travelers anymore.

Replacing the brilliant illumination of the fire's prime,
a few failing embers hid dejectedly behind the now thin wood,
indifferently sending their light through random windows
of space and small opaque panels of ravished log.

Finally, all that remained was the glow of the silent embers,
even those losing strength. logs still warm, chiminea still hot,
waiting to cool off and ready itself for the life of a future fire.

What does fire mean to you?

Forest Visit

*Inspired by Sophie Jupillat's musical prompt, **Low Temptation**. The piece begins slowly and moodily, gradually adding bits of louder and faster sounds. More moves are heard and the tonality is minor key in bass notes. Even slower sounds yet are heard, but in the forest the notes are combative and aggressive, indicating conflict and pain; they are now much faster. Sensitive listeners can picture themselves being chased.* **Try to match the musical activity to the word plot below OR imagine the music from the words in this visit.**

First, I amble randomly in the **park**,
my bare feet feeling the cool of the green grass
visiting briefly and nibbling between my soft toes.
It's late afternoon, but some gentle sunshine remains,
fairly bright but no longer hot.

Eventually, I exit the park,
returning to the slow-moving
laid back streets of the **city**.
I am in the company of other walkers,
several adults, a few children, and
a couple of dogs pretending they are lost.
I walk at a brisker pace than I did in the park,
almost trotting.

Suddenly fatigued, I sit down on a **bench**.
I am its only occupant.
Nearby benches support twos, threes, and even fours. . .
but not mine. That's fine with me
because I am not in the mood for company.
I notice the sun going down and
a light darkness spreading over the sky.
I feel my eyes close and I am anxious to return—
not to the park but to the **forest**, which I have visited before.

First, I am conscious of how much shorter I am
than the tall trees around me, many trees.
Very tall. With thick, dark brown branches,
all now curving in toward me, but not in a friendly way.
Wordlessly, they threaten me.
What did I do, I wonder, to be bullied this way?
I can't imagine. I realize that I must escape from the **forest**
but I have no sense of direction
or even an inkling of how I entered it.
I begin to run, or try to, but it is difficult
because I am swaying like the movement of the branches.
Now, the trees themselves are curving in toward me.

Finally I am able to run faster
and make some progress.
I feel lighter than I did before and a bit more nimble.
Still I remain in the **forest**,
treading on ground which, perhaps, I covered before.
The trees and branches are
coming closer and moving faster;
they make a whirring sound, like a maelstrom of sand.
Then they slow down and the noise nearly evaporates.
I, too, am moving more slowly now and
I envision myself returning to my **city** bench.
Will it still be there and available?

I open my eyes, blink, and find myself sitting on that same
bench. I look around in amazement.
The other benches are empty and evening has fully arrived.
The forest trees and their angry branches remain in
my thoughts and in my mind.
I feel safe now, but yet I miss the forest.
My forest.

LOVE STORIES

"Love means your soul has found its home."

— *Rita F. Dorn*

"If I had a flower for every time I thought of you... I could walk through my garden forever."

—*Alfred Lord Tennyson*

"When you realize you want to spend the rest of your life with somebody, you want the rest of your life to start as soon as possible."

—*When Harry Met Sally*

"Happy is coming to terms with life and its inflexible rules."

— *Rita F. Dorn*

Emily's Visit Home: A Variation

After Emily died in childbirth toward the end of Thornton Wilder's classic Our Town, *she ached for a chance to go back and see her family once more. The day she chose was her 11th birthday but was advised to select a less special day as the day would be become special enough because of her visit. During that encounter, she was invisible to her parents, but she could see and hear them. They were unaware of her or of her deeply emotional responses.*

In that vein, yesterday, driving home from my last day of the semester at the college where I teach, I was fondly recalling my beloved deceased parents; I fashioned a visit with them, envisioning them sitting side by side in my living room as I entered my home. My parents were seated comfortably on the sofa, greeting me warmly but calmly as I exuberantly, almost hysterically, hugged them back. Thrilled with this opportunity, of which I had many times dreamed, to catch them up on events in my life since their deaths and to ask them about their post death "lives," I totally basked in the thrill of this visit.

They looked pretty much as they had at their death ages, my dad at 82 in 1993 and my mother at 88 in 2000. My dad was dressed in one of the Florida senior citizen outfits he loved—color-coordinated slacks, sport shirt, and sox. My mom wore a cute pastel shorts and T-shirt set I had given her. They complimented the new living room furniture we had bought since their departures and told me I looked wonderful; I smiled gently, knowing i must have changed from late fifties to my seventies.

"Tell us about the boys," my mom requested.

I recounted how our older son had divorced his first wife of two years and moved to Brazil because he had fallen in love with a delightful Braziliana on his trip to Sao Paulo for a jujitsu tournament. He learned Portuguese quickly, pursued his lifetime passion for art and is now an internationally known artist, and "famous" as my dad, years earlier, had predicted he would be. I also told them about our younger son's speedy climb up the ladder of computer success with a major corporation and his love of extreme sports, as well as his recent marriage to a girl who shared that passion.

"Are their wives Jewish?" my mom asked, as I knew she would.

"No, they are not, but they are good people, and they love our boys!"

How could I have forgotten? I suddenly blurted out, "You have two great-grandchildren now!" and I grabbed the most recent photos of older son's 6-year old boy and 4-year old girl. "Oh, they are magnificent," my mom said wistfully. From her tone, I realized their visit would be brief and they would not get to meet the kids.

"And what about the two of you?" my dad asked, with a twinkle in his eye. I smiled at him, realistically acknowledging that his hair was white and had been for some years before his passing, but I had always seen it as the blond of his youth and my childhood.

"Well, your son-in-law has been retired for 11 years now and loves it, keeping himself active on boards of directors and with community projects, one of which was serving on a committee to turn the old Parrot Jungle park into an outdoor theatre."

"No racquet ball?" my mom asked facetiously, referring to their own athletics, in their 80's.

I recalled how my dad used to bike to the gym while my mom jogged the three-mile trip. "No, no racquetball for us," I replied, "but I, in my sixties. . ." and here I had to pause for emphasis, as I proudly continued. "I went back to college and got a master's degree in English, and now teach at the university."

They were duly impressed. This was their daughter, whom my high school dean, long ago, had advised them to send to secretarial school and not waste their money on university because "she is not college material." They congratulated me heartily, sincerely sharing my success, as only those who harbor genuine love and concern can.

"You both look great," I said truthfully, hugging them hard again and squeezing their hands.

"What about you?" I asked.

"Tell me about death. You have no idea how much I miss you both, every single day."

"Yes, we know," my mom said.

My dad added, "You come to the cemetery pretty often." I nodded somberly.

"Please tell me how you are and how you managed this fabulous visit. Oh, I am sooooo happy to see you. I can't believe it."

I kissed them both again, hard.

"How is death? Is there Heaven? Did you meet God? Tell me."

Gender Fluid & More

I am gender specific. Was a girl, am a woman.
Always have been and still am
clearly, comfortably, and confidently a female.
I never felt like a guy and do identify as a female,
all the time. So I guess I am not non-binary.

Not that I am criticizing chicks
who feel like guys some days of the week.

We are so living in a world where, every year,
more fences are coming down and
more boundaries are being deleted, —a good thing.

Born a girl? Don't have to hook up with guys;
other femmes are fair game. Or both. OK to be bi.
Born a girl? Don't have to wear frills.
Transvestites may now wear guy garb and vice versa.
Born a girl? Don't have to stay a girl.
Transition into becoming a male, if you wish.
Born a girl? OK to feel like a guy some days.

As for this girl, I don't feel like a guy. Ever.
Guess I am not gender fluid and that's fine.
Re: those who are, that's fine too.

Gender fluid, the newest addition to my vocabulary.

If I Had a Hammer, I'd. . . . .

If I were a dentist, I'd call my practice **Gentle Dental**
If I owned an antique shop, I'd name it **Past Tense**
If I owned a tile and carpet store, I'd call it **Floor Play**
If I had three daughters, I'd name them Chl**oe**, **Zoe**, and Ph**oe**be
My editing company would be **Semantic Makeovers**
If I led a choir in my hometown, we'd be the **Local Vocals**
If I taught people computer skills, I'd be the '**Puter Tutor**

The Cakery would be my bakeshop
A Pound of Round would be my butcher shop
Sew, What's New? would be my sewing shop
     or else **Nimble Thimble**
Nails and Pails would be my hardware store
Cool Pool Tools would be my pool supply outlet.
Pool School would be my swimming classes
Less Mess would be my cleaning company

Flower Power landscapers
Seeds & Weeds gardeners
Wong Two Tree quick organic Chinese take-out
Cat Naps & Yuppie Puppies pet spa
Math Path accountants
Bookie Cookie literary baker
Bright Lights night club
Deals on Wheels used car lot
Hiking and Biking outdoor supply store
Cutie Patootie little kids' clothing shop
Aware of Your Hair beauty salon
Beach Preacher outdoor sermons on the sand

Sitting in the London Airport Café, Etc.

Sitting in the <u>London</u> airport café, consuming croissants and espresso, I stare at the people here with me, all snuggled up to their carry-on luggage. Knowing we are bound for a multitude of world-wide destinations reminds me of a wheel whose millions of spokes are painted in different colors and pointed in different directions, radiating out across the globe.

Reflecting on the paintings and sculpture we viewed in the Louvre, I feel connected to history in a way I never did before. Reading about these people and places in books was a weak shot, in contrast to the passion and opulence of the "up-close and personal" of being here **<u>in</u> <u>Paris</u>** in the flesh. It makes me exquisitely conscious of my tiny part in the evolution of humanity.

The Blue Corduroy Chair

Dear Dad,

Your blue corduroy lazy boy reclining chair has lived in our house, lo, these years since mom passed away. From your death to hers, it graced her living room, regally holding court in a prominent corner.

I sit in it often; it now resides in my small, light blue walled home office. I never do so without thinking of you, of how many years you wanted such a chair, offering the ultimate in relaxing comfort, but how you never bought one until you were dying. You many times spoke of having such a chair. I do not know why you never bought one earlier.

I remember visiting you often in your house when you were sick. You sat in that chair but were not happy. I wish so much you had bought it earlier. I wish we had been sensitive enough to push you into getting it when you were hale and healthy, so you would've smiled sitting in that chair. You always looked sad and hopeless, waiting to die, when I saw you in it. I hugged you every time, trying to infuse some love and strength into your body.

The chair has been repurposed as Jeff and I both sit in it, alternately, he looking at internet news on his phone and I playing Scrabble on mine, in the blue corduroy chair. Your chair. It's so comfortable and welcoming to our bodies when they seek some physical comfort. The blue corduroy chair, your legacy to us. It still lives. And has your name on it. It speaks. "David," it says. I smile and wipe away a tear.

Love Your Libraries

Libraries are like a pot of gold, not at the end of a rainbow, but right in the middle of your own neighborhood!!

Think of all the riches they contain and give you as gifts, just for the asking; never a charge; you "pay" with your library card, which has no annual fee.

TRAVEL: Tickets take you to any place on the planet—nearby and familiar or distant; in space too. View the art, architecture, landscapes, industries, animals, and lifestyles. Experience far away cultures.

FOOD: Cookbooks offer you cuisine both exotic and familiar, plain or fancy, for a feast or a one bowl meal. For children's parties and lunch boxes. Gourmet or budget, pig-out or healthy, fuss or fast. Dinner, desserts, picnics, snacks.

NEW FRIENDS: Meet exciting people, in all fields, both living and dead, recent or historical, admirable or not, famous or infamous, well-known or less so. Politicians, rock-stars, nurses, religious leaders, dancers, athletes, trailblazers, and ordinary folks. The list of biographies and autobiographies is nearly endless.

CLASSES BUT NO TESTS: Learn how to do almost anything, work at your own pace, acquire knowledge about only what interests you. Close the book when you feel like it. You can now build a house, play the guitar, improve your dancing or your tennis game, take care of a sick kid or elderly granny, find a career, paint in oils or water color, repair an appliance. Research something. Hear DVDs without having to buy them. Learn French, *oui*?

ESCAPE: Leave your own life for awhile and live with the characters in a novel. Immerse yourselves in their environments, face their challenges with them, and try to solve their problems. Celebrate their joy. Think about them long after you read the last page. Visit the beauty of a poetry collection—powerful, dreamy, idealistic, stimulating, eye-opening.

EVENTS: Workshops, lectures, speakers, meetings, instruction, and groups are additional goodies to the book benefits, all friendly and all can be found in your local library.

"Why do all these things with a book instead of on the Internet?" you may ask. Well, turning the pages of a book gives you a personal connection to its contents. You can feel its history, maybe smell the ink, hear the voices of characters in a play in your own head. For the weeks during which it lives in your house, it is an invited guest, whom you welcome and respect, and interact with intermittently, repeatedly.

Furthermore, by patronizing your local library you not only enjoy the jewels of that bottomless pot of gold, but you are also preserving the history and revered tradition of libraries as a public service, available to everyone, a true symbol of a civilized society.

The Poem

of all the people in your life whom you meet, interact with, and move away from, there are always a few whom you can never ever forget. they hold an esteemed place in your heart, the ones about whom you can remember every detail, every conversation, every hug. you respected them then and also now, even though they no longer dwell in your life.

well, one of those people in my life was a man named marc. i met him when i was 25 and going through a tug-of-war divorce; that's a divorce where the participants can't make up their minds whether they want to get divorced or stay married and they keep canceling the court date. anyhow, what i noticed first about marc were his crinkly, twinkling eyes; i cannot recall what color they were but only how they sparkled when he smiled, which was often. also, i loved his confident but easy-going voice. that's a powerful combination: strength and softness. he was of medium height and wiry to medium build. marc was a financial vice president for a major oil company and a few years my senior. he was divorced, like me, and had a son; i inferred that his divorce had not been amiable. his ex-wife's first name is my middle name. he told me he'd had a pet bird who suddenly died one day, minutes before marc received a phone call from his mom to tell him that his dad had passed away. i related.

anyhow, we hit it off from the first minute: we admired the same poets, liked theatre way more than film, and frequented art museums.

he was articulate and we delighted in word-banter: puns, literary references, favorite quotes. we browsed bookstores, went to plays, and ate steak and baked potato dinners at miami's 1960's restaurants like gallaghers, hurricane harbor, and the studio. a few mornings, i cooked him breakfast in my apartment. he bought me poetry books, which we read together and speculated on what the authors' emotional triggers had been for each ode.

now one of my all-time, iron-clad requirements for the men i dated was that they be the same religion as I was; this was absolute, non-negotiable, 100%, no exceptions. marc wasn't and i didn't care. i wanted my parents, who lived nearby, to meet him to experience his wit and charm. so one afternoon, we dropped in on them, and had a short, warm, very pleasant visit. he asked about their lives and listed attentively to their replies. on the phone with me the next day, my mom said, "you are in love with him," which, of course, i hotly denied, insisting he was only a friend.

at some point, people in a relationship give thought to where it is going. i could envision being with marc every day for the rest of my forever—complete with myself and the world. i shared and absorbed all that he was. however, i knew before he verbalized it that permanence was not going to be one of our destinations. he once said, early on, "one of two things will happen: we'll become lovers for awhile or friends for awhile." i heard the word "awhile" clearly, but turned my back on it and refused to pay it any heed.

we dated for the rest of that year, both of us finding our time together rewarding: plays, concerts, sidewalk art shows, happy hours, rich conversation. as summer loomed, i decided to move from miami for a change of scenery and also because i was still seeing my now ex-husband—another relationship that wasn't going anyplace. without a computer, marc and i researched cities by requesting brochures from their chambers of commerce. the two finalists were boston and atlanta. i chose atlanta because its southern grace had always appealed to me and because it was closer to miami and my parents. i flew to atlanta to snag a teaching job for the next fall; i came home with no contract but with a renewed zest for life and huge enthusiasm for moving to *atlaaaaanta*. as that current school year ended, i crystallized my relocation plans.

it seems that marc had an ex-girlfriend who lived in atlanta, but taught at a college in macon during the week. she told marc i could stay in her apartment until i found one of my own. just like him to still be on good terms with an ex. is that not classy? he also gave me a few names of colleagues of his in the corporate sector in case i decided not to teach. i moved to atlanta, found my own place, got hired as a news reporter, and happily settled into single life in the south. we didn't really keep in touch, until he called me one day to tell me that he was getting married and invited me to the wedding—to the ex-girlfriend in whose apartment i had stayed during my first week in town. um, OK. i attended their nuptials at the unitarian church in atlanta and wished them well. soon later, i married jeffrey, my true (and still) soul mate, whom i had met three weeks after touching down on atlanta soil. shortly following the birth of our first son, we returned to miami for a new job for jeff and to let my parents glory in our baby.

i had and have a very good life with jeff; we welcomed another son, bought a house, did what people do, as their lives progress. one day, several years ago, i searched for marc on anywho and found him living in texas. on a whim, i called to say hello, unsure if he would remember me. his wife (the same one) answered the phone, recognized my name, greeted me warmly and said marc would love to speak to me. his familiar confident and sensuously stretched out voice sounded very pleased that i had called.

we chatted, catching up on the typical highlights of our lives. then he asked if i still wrote poetry. "of course i do, and i teach it at my college." he said, "you wrote a poem for me once. hold on. i'll go get it." what? i had no recollection of writing a poem for him, but i was touched that he had kept it and astonished that he could find it! sure enough, he returned to the phone with the short poem, which he read to me. i still didn't recall it but i did recognize my poetic style. the call was a success and now we exchange holiday greeting cards, with updates of our careers, surgeries, and travels.

everyone we meet leaves a thumbprint on our hearts; some prints fade before the person has even walked away; others remain forever. i knew marc had left a mark on me, but his keeping that poem must mean that i had left a small mark on him too.

EPILOGUE: *carl f. marquardsen passed away from throat cancer a few years later. his wife still keeps in touch with me.*

How She Learned to Love Sleeping Naked

When they first began sleeping together, she came to bed wearing a frilly little nightgown which she hoped he would find very sexy.

Instead, he grumbled, "Why are you wearing that overcoat?"
"I'm cold," she answered.
"Cold?" he said. "What kind of cold? It's not snowing here."

Eventually, on nights when she thought he would want to make love or on nights which she hoped they would, she climbed into bed, bare. He always verbalized his appreciation, proclaiming the importance of letting skin breathe, unencumbered, respite from the labor of carrying clothing around on it all day.

Sometimes she did it just as a treat for him, even if they didn't engage. He stroked her, gently, affectionately. It was pleasant.

Then, one night when he was out of town, she got into bed naked, alone, just for herself. Sweet. Liberating. Slightly sexy but relaxing. And she could almost feel her skin breathing. Conscious of her smooth body pressed upon the delicately rough surface of the sheets, she took sensory joy in the contact. She felt like a little baby, totally at peace.

When he returned from his business trip the next afternoon, she reported to him her newfound delight in sleeping in the buff, for herself as well as for him.

"It's about time," he said.

Then he asked with a devilish smile, "Want to take a nap?"

Gangs Aren't Such Bad People

When our son was living in New York in the mid 1990's while going to college, he and his friends often came home late from weekend parties, walking on the streets of Brooklyn.

One evening Tobin and a few buddies were doing that. Seeing a hostile looking group slowly approach them, one pal poked our son and said in a panicky voice, "Look! It's a gang. Let's get out of here!"

Son answered, "A real gang? I never saw one before!" The friends were ready to take flight when Son said, "Hey, they are all wearing the same leather jackets!"

The posse was now close; Son walked right up to them said, "Are you guys a gang?"
The leader answered in an intimidating tone and with a fearsome look in his eyes, "Yeah, what about it, jerk?"
Son answered, "And you all have the same jackets!"
The leader said, "Yeah. You're a real genius. So what?"
Our son, always focused, replied, "But you don't have a logo for the jackets!!"

The leader and a few others asked, "What the Hell is a logo?"

Now enthused and oblivious to his own friends' discomfort at hanging out so long with these hoods, Tobin said, "A design that goes on your jackets to show you're members of this gang. What's the name of your gang, anyhow?"

"Why do you want to know?" asked one of them. Cautious but interested, the leader told the name of their gang.

Now fully in his element, Tobin said, "I'm an artist and I can paint logos on your jackets for you. Give me one and I'll meet you back right here next week with the logo on it. Same time."

The leader conferred with a few others. Son could see their hesitation. One guy said to him, "Yeah, right. We're supposed to give you an expensive leather jacket when we don't even know you? Forget it, kid!"

"No," Son said, showing them his college ID card with his address and photo. "I'll bring it back with a logo. If you don't like it, don't pay me. If you do, I can illustrate all your jackets." They briefly discussed the graphic our son proposed, depicting the gang's name, and finally handed over a jacket.

The leader leaned close to Tobin's face and said in a gruff, threatening voice, "If you don't show up, we will come and get you. That's a promise. They'll never find your body!"

"No sweat. I'll be here. Goodnight." Tobin and his crew continued back to campus, the friends astounded at what had just taken place. Tobin happily tucked the jacket under his arm.

EPILOGUE: *The gang members loved their new logo; Tobin did one a week for eight weeks at $200 per jacket. So now some gang members are cruising around Brooklyn, wearing our son's artwork on their jackets. Tobin's comment about it: "Gangs aren't such bad people after all, and they appreciate art!!"*

Travel Agent

array-cation	many choices
away-cation	far off
bay-cation	on the water (fishing, boating)
bray-cation	on a ranch with horses (or neigh-cation)
clay-cation	ceramics
day-cation	24 hours (a quickie)
dray-cation	travel by cart or horse-drawn wagon
fray-cation	unraveled
gay-cation	rainbow family
hay-cation	on the farm
jay-cation	for lovers of blue birds
May-cation	springtime celebration
nay-cation	negative
oy vey-cation	Jewish
play-cation	board games, cards, Mah Jong
pray-cation	religious retreat
ray-cation	for sun-worshippers; bring sunscreen
slay-cation	dragon themes; take your favorite sword
spay-cation	volunteer at the local animal shelter
stay-cation	extended
tray-cation	gourmet food
weigh-cation	weight loss, healthy
whey-cation	dairy spa, as in "curds and. . . "

WAR STORIES

"Never have a battle of wits with an unarmed person."
— *Mark Twain*

"An eye for an eye will only make the whole world blind."
—*Mahatma Ghandi*

"Literature is a war against cliche."
—*Martin Amis*

"Fleeing pain and chasing comfort"
— *R. F. Dorn*

How do They Know?

I once heard my school principal lavishly extol my teaching skills to several other faculty and some visiting brass, praising my classroom management skills to the skies.

After about a half hour of discussion, the new psychologist I was seeing, on hearing that I was a writer, referred to the "great works" I had written.

My son and his recent bride joined us and a group of our friends at a local restaurant for dinner; they went around the table, Son introducing new wife as they went. After they left, one of the women referred to son's wife as "your wonderful daughter-in-law."

Everybody likes to hear compliments, but I have a problem with the ones above. What is my problem? Answer: the principal had not once observed me in the classroom, the psychologist had not read anything I wrote, and our friend had no way of knowing if the new daughter-in-law was, indeed, "wonderful." People who make and verbalize their baseless assumptions, with no evidence, should not be surprised if the recipients of the praise are not overjoyed.

I did not pursue the issue with the principal because he was, after all, my current boss, and I figured it would behoove me to leave that one alone. Perhaps he was trying to strengthen his own professional image in hiring competent staff. On the other hand, I smiled pleasantly at the psychologist and asked her innocently, "Oh, have you read any of my pieces?" Sheepishly, she admitted that she had not, but merely assumed that I was a fine writer. . . .which I certainly like to think I am, but that's not the point. The person who called my new daughter-in-law "wonderful" was my friend's out of town relative, who, I'm sure, was just trying to be pleasant to me.

OK, so why am I doing all of this complaining? Would I have preferred the principal to tell the group that I was sometimes late to school? That was something about which he knew. No, of course not. The psychologist, though, could have asked me what kind of material I wrote and said, "You seem to love writing." The word, "seem" would protect her because, unless I had verbalized my love for writing as well as my engagement in it, which (although true) I had not, she would have been safe in stating this judgment as her observation. My friend's relative, as well, could have taken refuge in "seems to be" or "appears to be," since she had never met the young woman before. All she knew was what she saw: Your daughter-in-law "is very pretty,"(her opinion. OK) "has a gentle voice,"(opinion. OK) "wore a beautiful green dress," (beautiful is opinion and green is a (fact. OK) or "told me she comes from Idaho —how interesting!" (fact. OK) would have been better choices.

So what is my point here? My point is that people should say what is documentable, if they want it to be credible, rather than presenting as fact content about which they really do not know. They should not verbalize assumed content about which they do not know for sure and which others may realize they don't. Furthermore, they should be more precise in their word selection, aiming for accuracy. Alternate comment from the principal: "Mrs. Dorn has been teaching here for several years and we all think highly of her." Complimentary but not too specific, true, and within his range of knowledge. Language is a melody, which we should all try to sing, on key.

A Double Standard: Don't Judge Me

Many people, currently, want unconditional love, endless chances, do-overs, some slack cut, and breaks. They clamor for no rules, no boundaries, no restrictions, zero consequences, and total freedom to do as they please, even if their actions step on someone else's toes; they lobby for eligibility to collect unconditional love, despite their ugly, damaging behavior.. . . because it is supposed to be unconditional, and available to all.

When we do good things, achieve colossal heights, and accomplish notable deeds, we want to be judged and have our just due bestowed on us: awards, rewards, raises, praise, prizes, jackpots, good grades, and abundant benevolence from all corners. Why, then, do so many ask not to be judged? Ah, they don't ask to be unjudged all the time, but only when they break the rules of society, the law, and groups. They shun their accountability. They want a double standard.

Therefore, a societal spokes voice should reply to those who demand not to be judged, "On which deeds do you want judgment lifted? On all of your deeds? The good ones too or just the ones which would bring you recriminations and criticism? If you are not judged on some, you lose the ability to be judged on the others. It's all or nothing. You can't have it both ways."

As far as receiving unconditional love, that means you get it no matter what your conduct is, right? Because it is unconditional, it is not contingent on earning it or on your worthiness. In that case, perhaps teachers should give all students A's, whatever their academic performance. And bosses should give all workers raises and promotions, regardless of their level of productivity. And all parents should praise their children constantly, whether they behave well or badly, thereby providing them unconditional love. Right? If that is the case, then what is this unconditional love worth? If available to all, then its value plummets to nothing. If there are no levels of performance required to get it, what is the point of giving anybody anything? Not much. Such love has the same worth as a prize in a Cracker Jacks box.

Thus, if everyone gets the same salary, the same grade, and the same love, where is the role of competition? What is the point of trying to do one's best? Competition, which spurs many on to create items of life-changing value, would disappear and, so, soon, would progress.

The next time a person demands, "Don't judge me," reply "Are you sure?" or "Exactly which deeds don't you want judged?" or "All of them, the pristine (which produce benefits) or the disreputable ones (which bear consequences)?" Judgment must be consistent. Possibly, those opposing judgment, in the face of one policy for all deeds, will clean up their acts, knowing their acts will be dealt with by a single standard across the board. No more double standards. And no more unconditional love; it should be conditional, based on recipient worth.

How Does it Feel to Have a Sibling Die?

Sad, abandoned, miserable, incorrect, fervently wishing I could turn back the clock. Not real, a nightmare, a void, a gap, a precious part of my life missing, having been jaggedly ripped out.

My younger brother, Eric, passed away when he was 63 and I was 67. He had been diagnosed with mantle cell leukemia following surgery for a benign brain tumor four months earlier. Survival time for MCL is estimated at 2-5 years, and my good friend, Carole, a nurse, assured me that "someone has to reach five years." After the operation, it was decided that he should have radiation, which his close friend, Ron, a physician, advised against because it sometimes strengthens leukemia, but Eric took it anyhow. He pretty much denied his condition, not being able to face his own mortality, and tried to go on about his life as if he were not ill and at risk. His girlfriend, Sheila, kept reminding him to be careful, but he cheerfully ignored her. We all cautioned him, but to no avail. We worried.

So how did/does it feel— then, since, now? Abandoned. Beyond dreadful. Cold. Spooky, scary, dark, sad, very sad. He and I shared a deep foundation of love, family, and closeness despite surface conflicts, of which there were many. I never thought he would die first because I was the older one. I could not begin to anticipate how this would feel.

The pain still goes away briefly and comes back with a vengeance, all the time, every day, many moments and many minutes, in depth. I feel bad for me but worse for him.

It feels like an important part of my childhood, adulthood, and life have been retracted—a part that I thought belonged to me, unconditionally and permanently. After our parents died, Eric and I always spoke on the phone on their birthdays, *yahrzeits*, and wedding anniversary. Together, we recalled the good moments we had shared with them, humorous stuff they said, and frequent advice they gave. We often referred to people Eric and I knew as children and in college when one of them would cross our paths. Often only he and I shared those friendships or knew those people. Eric and I were the only ones who knew the silly song we composed and sang in the bathtub together as little kids.

Eric was a party-animal, joke-teller, fact-checker, gift-giver, artist, musician, traveler, adventurer, dog-lover, a wild child, film buff, and chocolate chip cookie eater, who wanted to get his money's worth out of his life and he did. So many people will remember him with positive images. As my son Tobin wrote for Eric's memorial, "My Uncle Eric did pretty much everything he wanted to. Not many people can say that." He devoted himself 100% to each thing that he attempted—jobs, trips, relationships. My son Corey spoke at length about his Uncle Eric, citing that he was deep, generous, cheerful, and sensitive. He left his mark on a vast number of people. We have the photos and the memories but they are not enough. He loved being a son, a brother, a brother-in-law, an uncle, a boyfriend, a buddy, and a friend.

This is so different from when our parents passed away because we always knew we would see that. I feel vulnerable. I did not expect this, even after he got sick. Guess I do some denial too. I often recall our childhood together and the many golden times, funny things that we said and did, family vacations taken, games played in our big backyard, loud whispering between our bedrooms after the lights were out, all kinds of stuff, good stuff, not invisible but definitely faded now, with a gloomy haze over it all. A wrong that cannot be corrected. I hate it and miss him so much. I try to feel grateful that he was in my life as long as he was, but I feel more sad that he is no longer here. It hurts, a lot. Like a punch in the face, chest, heart, and soul, all at once. Still. That's how it feels, for me, to have a sibling die. My only sibling.

The Day I Stopped Loving You

In my third year of teaching, I became friends with two other teachers, who were going through painful, messy, nasty divorces; this is a composite of their stories. They vented to me often and I listened.

i don't exactly remember the day i stopped loving you;
maybe it was a process, a parade of continuous little
hammer taps on the edge of the china of our relationship,
each of them leaving a small dent, chip, or scratch,
until finally it didn't look good anymore. it certainly could no longer be used.

it seemed like the process took a long time, and we were
aware of it happening, at least i was. maybe you did not know until it was over and done, when it could not be rescued anymore, although for many months we still behaved as if survival were a possibility. we both gave it lip service, words positive and upbeat, but always hollow, at least to me.

and then one day it could no longer be denied or ignored.
i slowly removed my wide gold wedding band and placed it on the mirrored perfume tray on my dresser. i heard the small clink it made.....i stared at it there for several seconds and for several more seconds, maybe a whole minute, and then i picked it up, opened my seventh floor apartment window, and with vengeance, threw it out, quickly closing

the window, not waiting for it to reach the cement below. I felt it was like a stone being thrown into the depths of the ocean.

that wasn't the day i stopped; that was just the retiring of the official symbol of our marriage, the ring. the actual day was much, much earlier, maybe even way before the hammer began to tap the side of the plate. hard to say.

when did it all begin to die? i'm not perfectly sure of that either. maybe it was when i came home from school early one afternoon and found you and your pretty, young secretary in our bed. you hurriedly ushered her out and swore up and down that this was a mistake, a one-time error never to be repeated, no need for it to be repeated because we really had a good marriage, you said.

hmm, well, perhaps. or maybe it was when a significant amount of money disappeared from our joint checking account and you insisted it was a bank error on which you were working with them to correct. you worked on it for a very long time and i don't clearly recall it ever reaching a satisfactory resolution.

or maybe it was the business conference you attended in another city, never answering the phone when i called you but always returning my call in a respectable amount of time with a pat explanation of precisely where you had been and what you had been doing. you reminded me how much we both wanted you to advance in your company.

perhaps it was the day i saw you and a preppy co-worker/buddy lunching at an upscale restaurant where my cousin had taken me for a surprise birthday meal. you were tightly holding his hands in yours on the table, your glances locked, both of you oblivious to the rest of the world. i did not confront you until that evening at home (very stupid of me) when you totally denied the entire incident, saying that i was mistaken, it had not been you, and how could i have even thought of such an outrageous thing? you said that you were shocked and highly insulted by such an accusation.

possibly it was the night you were "working late" and did not come home until the next morning, drunk, disheveled, disoriented, not even exerting yourself to create an excuse of any sort. you angrily rebuked my later attempts to reopen that discussion or revisit that time, as i tried to clear the air and get some closure.

bizarrely enough, interspersed with these flagrant red flags were some great conversations filled with seemingly sincere and sensitive words, a few fun trips, generous gifts from you, and some decent sexual encounters. how could i have even bothered? one day i realized that a change was long overdue. i faced the fact that whatever lay ahead for me had to be better than what i was living with and that death was not the only thing qualified to do us part.

precisely when the music stopped, i still don't know. most people could probably identify when they first fell in love but would be hard pressed to pinpoint just when that love expired. the end of anything else (other than a novel, a piece of music, or a school semester) is not usually a moment, but more like the result of a very gradual process, one that quietly sneaks up on us. and then it's done.

the wedding ring? well, that was just the discarding of the symbol of something that no longer existed and, thus, had no more purpose.

Care / Don't Care.
(Follow The Dots, If You Can)

Two people can argue and still care about each other. They can yell, cry, threaten, say hurtful things, and still care. They can vote differently and follow different religions, and still care. They can refuse to answer a few phone calls and ignore a few texts and emails, and still care. When they don't talk, text, or email for awhile but see each other regularly or reliably, maybe that's OK; they might still care. But when they don't talk, don't text, don't email, don't visit, it's not OK. When they are not moved by the emotions or pain of the other, then they absolutely cannot still care.

What can be done about someone who does not care (or no longer cares) about you? Probably nothing. If one forces the other into a conversation (to clear the air, sort things out, talk it through, get closure, whatever), it will most likely not end in a satisfying way for the uncared about person. How can an individual stop caring about someone for whom one once had meaningful feelings? Well, that's a whole other story, with a complex multitude of possibilities. Caring is fragile, mysterious, elusive, an inconstant entity —without concrete start and stop dates. And yet we tend to view it as an irrefutable constant in our lives. A given. It's not.

Why Do Students Cheat on Tests?

Six "good" reasons: notice the mnemonic, IF GLAD.

INSECURITY- They have **no confidence** that their own ability is sufficient to perform well, assuming that someone else's work will be superior to their own. They view themselves as poor students who are unable to improve, even with help from tutors, teachers, parents, and/ or friends.

FEAR- They are **fearful of negative consequences** from parents, teacher, peers, the student loan committee, college admissions, and/or the scholarship board in response to a low grade. They also fear their own self-condemnation for not doing well.

GREED- They **lust for a better grade** than what they think they could possibly achieve on their own and reach out for that golden apple, seeing only the glory and ignoring the risk.

LAZINESS- They are **too lazy** to do the prescribed work, even though many teachers and professors cut the big assignment into bite size pieces, each to be done in a small time frame, so as not to overwhelm their students. These pupils don't like to study and refuse to force themselves to do so, even ignoring easy, helpful opportunities for assistance.

AVAILABILITY- Easy to come by. A classmate's paper is within eyeshot, essays are conveniently for sale on the internet, a buddy is amenable to writing a pal's term paper, and a friend who took the test earlier willingly shares questions and answers.

DESPERATION- They have procrastinated, waiting until the last minute, when it is no longer probable that they can do an adequate job on the assignment by themselves. They are now, although late, **desperate to get a decent grade** on this work.

These are the same reasons that adults "cheat," i.e. commit illegal or criminal acts. They are convinced that they cannot excel by following honest pathways, and that "cheating" is their only option to achieve "success" (monetary or performance). Dishonest adults and students tell themselves, "everyone does it" or "it's no big deal," in attempt to justify their misconduct. Young people often do the same, convincing themselves that it is OK. Many, as they mature, come to the realization that it was not OK and decide to take another path, the high road. Kudos to them for growing up and out of their youthful indiscretions!

Mnemonic: IF GLAD
> **I**nsecurity
> **F**ear
>
> > **G**reed
> > **L**aziness
> > **A**vailability
> > **D**esperation

Waiting

it seems that all my life i have been waiting for one thing or another. when i was a child, i recall waiting to become a teenager. i impatiently thought that childhood was lasting too long (i now see the folly in that). as a teen, i waited again, anticipating going to college. once there, of course, i waited to graduate and have my first job. then i was waiting to fall in love and get married. naturally, the next wait was to have a baby and buy a house. we furnished the house and waited for our two sons to grow. we watched them do so and waited for them to finish school. when they did and got their first jobs, we waited for them to fall in love and get married, which they did, as well. naturally, we next waited for grandchildren to appear.

four lovely ones have done so.

both boys are grown up and out now and successfully on their own and we, as the parents, are living in the house we love, and waiting for . . . . what? one of us is retired and the other semi-retired— the golden years we waited for all the decades that we worked are upon us. but now, we wait, from week to week, for one social engagement after another; but those, while pleasant, are thin, neither compelling nor urgent. the earlier "waiting-fors," as i look back, seemed bigger, more important, more necessary, more real. they were genuine, rather than contrived or artificially formed. we see some friends dying and others becoming ill. are we waiting to dodge death and sidestep serious illnesses? are we examining ourselves for signs of cancer, dementia, and the other boogie-men which attack survivors of youth and middle age? are we just subconsciously waiting for one of us to die, to see who will be first? what are we waiting for now?

as impatient as i was to jump into the next earlier slices of my life, which always dangled before me like a carrot in front of the rabbit, motivating me to run faster, now i feel at a loss with no real carrot in sight. it's sobering to realize that, as good as we feel (most of the time) and as good as we look (which we think is pretty good), we are definitely in Part III, with Part I-Beginning and Part II-Middle having been completed. typical advice is "Don't think about it—just enjoy each today! and don't squander even a minute." OK, but why? because these days are numbered and winding down way faster than they spiraled upward? yes, of course, that is the reason. when i did the earlier "wait-fors," it was luxurious to look ahead to not only the next one but to the abundance of those beyond the then-current one. not so today.

yes, life is easier now, less pressure, less stress, less need to compete, but to what avail? at what cost is this more leisurely walk? i'm not only at loose ends because my "wait-fors" are unarguably fewer, but because i'm surprised at my missing the structure, the thrust, the impetus and strength of the years which led up to this one. i think i will have to create some powerful new "nexts" and force myself to believe in their authenticity. i still need something genuine to wait for, even now.

A Broken Sound

How can a sound be broken? It can be interrupted, that is, stopped before completion, but broken?

Like broken in half? So it doesn't work any more? What work does a sound do? Its only work is being itself, to be expressed as a vibration heard by ears.

What is a non-broken sound? Most of them are. And we take their wholeness for granted, expecting it as our due.

But to break it or hear it be broken? Can someone break it or must it be broken from some other source?

A piece of music halted mid sound. A word truncated before all syllables are out in the open. A broken spoken word. What a shame.

POTPOURRI

"Do not struggle to be appreciated by others; learn to appreciate yourself."

—Unknown

"Life is potpourri; love is its fragrance."

—Anonymous

"What lies behind us and lies ahead of us are tiny matters compared to what lies within us.,"

—Ralph Waldo Emerson

Being There

"being there" used to mean being present at a particular location at a particular time. it was in contrast to not being there or to being someplace else. pretty simple.

now, however, "being there for" someone seems to imply being fully available, on duty, maybe 24/7, and certainly whenever that someone is in need. "in need" could be a dire emergency like coming to the hospital to share his or her angst when a loved one is in critical condition. it could be lending or giving him or her money or a ride or a necessary object.

on the perhaps less urgent but equally important part of the "being there spectrum" is providing a sounding board or a shoulder to lean on or cry on. a person who has always been there is one of the most greatly appreciated individuals, as in "he has always been there for me" or "I was there for her" the "there" meaning of course where, when, and however long the needy person is in emotional need. not only physically present.

Sex and The Grammar Lesson

Perhaps you recall grammar lessons on adjectives and adverbs from elementary school; perhaps you don't. Anyhow, here is a vocabulary update on adjectives for the noun, "sex."

NON-MARITAL SEX: Sex with no interest in marriage from either party, now or ever. Friends with benefits or possibly not even friends, just beneficiaries. Maybe sexmates.

PRE-MARITAL SEX: You are in love, you are going to get married, but you are having sex with him/her now; dress rehearsals or undressed rehearsals.

MARITAL SEX: Legal, proper, convenient; boring or keeps getting better as your relationship grows.

EXTRAMARITAL SEX: Sex with your lover and with your spouse (separately); best of both worlds?

POST-MARITAL SEX: Sex with your ex. If he/she had been this good in bed when you were married, you two might still be together.

Jack in The Box

It was my first year of middle school, but back
then we called it junior high.

Elementary had not been great, even though every
year I told myself the next one would be better; it
never was. The night before every first day of school,
my mother told me, "Jack, this is going to be a banner
year for you!" She smiled at me and said it like she
believed it. I scowled because I knew better.

Teachers didn't like me, I guess, because I wasn't
smart. I tried but could never seem to understand the
homework very well and so tests were a disaster. The
kids always found something to tease me about. One
year it was "Oh, Jack, you're so black," even though I
am white. Another year it was "Jack, Jack, go stand in
the back." Seventh grade was the worst. They called
me "Jack Ass." And then they added "Jack Ass, he won't
pass!" It was dreadful; I hated to wake up on school days.

But then, for seventh grade English, I had a very
nice teacher. She was young and seemed to like me.
She was patient and explained the work to me, even
asking me to come back after school for some help,

without the other kids watching. Her name was Miss
Violin. I once asked her if she knew how to play the
violin, but she just laughed and said, "No, I don't."

I really tried to do well in her class, but my
attention span was short, and after a few minutes I
could not even sit at my desk without wanting to
fidget. Of course, we were not allowed to get up and
walk around. One day when I arrived, I saw a big
cardboard box in the back of the room. I bent over to
peek in, and just then another kid came along and
pushed me into it. Plop!

At first I was angry, but then I looked around and
liked sitting in the box, so I stayed there. When Miss
Violin took attendance and called my name, I decided
not to answer because I was feeling so mellow in that
warm, restful, friendly cardboard box. The other kids
told her, "He's back there in that box." Miss Violin
came to the back of the room and looked in; I smiled at
her and asked if I could stay there for a few minutes.
"OK. I guess so," she said, "but are you all right?" I said I was.

She finished taking attendance and began to teach.
I could hear every word she said and seemed to absorb
the lesson well because I felt relaxed and not distracted.
After a while, I stood up, climbed out of the box and went to
my seat to sit down. I felt very good the rest of the day.

The next day, I went to my seat in English class,
but after a while I felt restless and asked Miss Violin
if I could go to the box for a few minutes. She looked
surprised but said I could. After a bit, I came out and
returned to my seat. The third day, some of the kids
started teasing me and punching me; Miss Violin was

writing on the board, and when she turned around, she only got to see me retaliate. She asked me if I wanted a few minutes in the box and I said, "Yes." So it went on that way. Either Miss Violin asked me to go in the box when she noticed me drifting or else I just went in myself. It was a welcome refuge from the other kids and also from feeling restless. In the meantime, Miss Violin's after school tutoring was bringing my grades up. I decided that I liked English class very much.

One day, after I had not slept well the night before, I was feeling drowsy, so I walked back to "my box." Lately, the other kids did not seem to be harassing me as much and I was understanding the work better too. I stayed in the box for quite some time and then stood up to return to my seat when I saw the principal, Miss Less, standing in the doorway. She was a severe looking woman – very tall, very thin and very old, with white hair pulled back into a bun. She often came to observe classes for a few minutes. I had no idea that when Miss Less appeared, Miss Violin began to pray that I would remain in the box until she left. When Miss Less saw me rise from that box, her eyes grew wide and her thin lips got tight. She began to tremble slightly. Then she looked angrily at Miss Violin and said in a low voice, almost a hiss, "Come to my office immediately after this class!"

Well, our English lesson continued, and I went on with the rest of my day. I don't know what happened between Miss Violin and Miss Less in the office, but the next day, my box was gone!

I missed that box very much, but was afraid to ask Miss Violin what had happened to it. I didn't know where it went, why it was taken away, or how it had gotten there in the first place. My mom said it probably had been left there, by mistake, by the janitor, and originally held paper towels or something.

Occasionally a kid would say something stupid to me like, "Hit the sack, Jack!" I just shrugged my shoulders and it did not bother me; somehow my classmates did not seem all that interested in teasing me anymore. I guess the cycle had been broken. That box was the ancestor of the modern Time Out Method that many teachers successfully use now.

EPILOGUE:

The rest of 7th grade without the box? Basically, I was a little bit more self-confident. I still got restless occasionally in class, but not that often, and when I did, I would just envision that box and pretend I was in it. Miss Violin continued to tutor me after school most of the year, until I really didn't need it any more. Then we stopped.

I was still not a genius or Mr. Popularity, but by the end of the year, two important changes had taken place. I got a B in English —my first B ever— and….I got a girlfriend, my first one of those also! She used to say to me, smiling, "Jack, Jack, you lead the pack!" or "Jack, you're right on track!" Yeah, I guess 7th grade ended up pretty good after all! And Mom was right. It <u>was</u> my banner year!

Layers

Layers of light
layers of love
layers of melancholy
layers of disappointment
layers of despair
layers of light shine through the despair
and go back into hiding.

Layers of love
hibernating in the coves of gloom
layers of energy
layers of ambition
layers of hope torn by dismay.

Layers of hope
wanting to survive.
layers of love
lying around, unused
layers of time: minutes, days, months, years
racing away.

Layers of light
cover me gently
as I toss restlessly
yearning for comfort.

Labels

We label those we meet, based on a wide variety of criteria.

We meet a Muslim, a Jew, a Catholic, an atheist, a Buddhist, and we make a judgment.

We meet a vegetarian, fruititarian, or carnivore, and we judge.

We meet someone from Alabama, New York, California, Brazil, the Netherlands, or Farmsville, Ohio, and we make a judgment.

We meet a lesbian, transgender individual, gay man, bisexual person, straight one, and we label them.

We talk to a child, a teen, a 30-40-50-something or elderly folks; we label them based on age.

We see those with more education than we have, some education, or no education and we categorize them, often on how close their educational level is to ours, or how different.

Encountering people with more money or less money than we have, we judge.

Crossing paths with people who had the same experiences we did, or contrasting ones, we connect or we separate—but we label them.

Meeting folks with similar or opposing political views? We sure do label them.

But ultimately, the similarities are greater than the differences…… hopefully.

We all cry at a loss, feel for those we care about who are facing hard times, are blue if the rough roads are our own, are profoundly sad when Death takes a loved one, experience hurt when disappointed, offended, or betrayed.

Thrill at the birth of a baby, at a romantic connection, at a personal or professional success, feel grateful when a health threat is overcome, feel excitement at a financial win.

The labels may be diverse but the joys are universal. If only we could focus on the similarities, on the labels that match!

Masks of Ourselves

Who are we when we look in the mirror,
when we meet friends and family or
acquaintances, colleagues, or rivals?

Are we the same person all the time or do we change?
Of course we change.
For each occasion we wear a different hat, cloak, and mask. . .
because for each event or audience, we play a different role, serve a
different function. Even have different voices and scripts.

It is important to be proud of our actions in every capacity.
Are we wearing the mask to hide behind or
just to assume an alternate identity?
For the occasion, for fun, for deception? To escape?

When we dress up in costumes,
we temporarily take on the identity of
the person whose clothes we are wearing, but
does good guy garb make us heroes?
Does a villain costume make us evil?

Do we use the masks of our lives to show another identity
rather than to conceal our flaws
or to give a deceptive impression?

Do we feel just as safe when we take off the mask
and look in the mirror, as when we wear it?

What are the real purposes of daily and holiday masks we wear?
A vacation from our everyday selves? A fantasy ID?
Revelation? A secret longing?
Food for thought.

They Call it by Many Names

"Move forward. Get over it. Let it go. Don't worry about it any more. It's over and done with. Go with the flow. Start fresh. Forget it. Forge ahead. Doesn't matter now. It was long ago."

Whatever else it's called, it's still the "Bury your head in the sand syndrome." Trying to believe that if you can't see it, it can't see you. Ignoring something that is not over but pretending it is, making believe that it isn't there anymore. Assuming the mantle of everything is OK, when, in truth, everything is not the least bit OK. As a matter of fact, nothing is OK. And furthermore, everything is majorly not OK.

But relative to the huge elephant in the small living room around whom everyone dances, not admitting he is in their house, this, too, is easy to view as invisible. . . . .as long as it is not your living room and not you trying to make peace with the elephant to avoid getting him all riled up.

It's like the fairy tale of <u>The Emperor's New Clothes</u>, and the emperor to whom nobody wanted to say, "You are stark naked. You are wearing neither new clothes, old clothes, nor any other kind of clothes." (A small child finally did.) Nor would they confess his nudity to each other. Why not? First of all, emperors, like other royalty, were known to have a messenger who brought bad news killed, forgetting he was only the bringer and not the author. Second, the tailors whom the emperor had hired were con men who stole the fine cloth and thread given to them to sew new clothes for the emperor but warned everyone that only wise people would be able to see the clothes; fools would not. Third, people feared admitting the emperor's nudity to each other, lest the emperor learn a speaker's identity and become so angry that he would have him killed as well. Better not to take a chance. . . .take a chance on what? On rocking the boat. Don't rock the boat, let sleeping dogs lie, "if it's not broke, then don't fix it—" because you might make it worse. Except that it IS broken and nobody, like the lack of a volunteer to bell the cat, wants to admit that it is broken and nobody will have any peace until it is fixed. No one wants to bell the cat who might bite the beller, even though he truly needs to be belled.

That being said, if one squeezes a pimple, he is forcing the pus to come out and be seen. Eww, gross. The pimple must then be wiped clean of the infected pus with a tissue, the tiny orifice blotted to stop any blood that wants to exit, and antiseptic must be applied with a cotton ball. Assuming there is no more pus inside, which, if there is, will not disappear but will expand to form another swollen pustule very soon; now, having been emptied of toxins, it is possible to start over. Why only now? Because now the skin is totally clean and not hiding any snipers.

However, just as complexion given to eruptions may have many pimples which must be emptied, disinfected, and permitted to start the healing process, relationships need the same kind of thorough treatment. They, too, can harbor numerous poisonous issues, which must be each excised and disposed of satisfactorily before healing can even think of starting its work.

So why do so many people wait so long, in the lonely and profound despair of silence before spilling the beans and opening the floodgates to reveal the truth? Because they are afraid. Afraid to rock the boat, afraid of the elephant's wrath, afraid of the emperor's ire, afraid of the opponent's fury and/or of their peers' disapproval? Honestly, some elephants and emperors will indeed kill the messenger; that's a risk that must be faced, because without extraction there can be no hope of peace, much less pleasure in this relationship. If fury results, it often subsides; even if it doesn't, at least everyone knows where he or she stands. Elephants do not make good roommates or good tenants or good guests; nor does pus.

Noah and The Ark: (*Fictionalization*)

So God gave **Noah** the word that a huge flood was coming and that he should start building an ark, inviting two of each species to embark with him. Obediently, Noah made a list of the supplies he would need and then went to Home Depot to buy them. He also posted on Craig's List a request for builders to help him and, on his website, invited two of each species to apply to join him, in exchange for a free, all-inclusive, extended cruise. Shortly, the construction team was working diligently, keeping in mind the deadlines that Noah had set for them. Soon, the ark was completed and ready for inhabitants. It was spacious, well-appointed, and comfortable. Chefs were engaged to feed the animals, recreation directors to entertain the population, nautical technicians to keep the ark afloat, and veterinarians to ensure the health of all. Noah alerted his wife, **Pearl**, that their departure date was coming close.

Many pairs of animals showed up for the free cruise. Two sleek tigers, Isabela and Oswaldo, appeared and Noah accepted them. Two strong grizzly bears, Monique and Pierre, showed up and were welcomed. Two regal lions, Linda and Leonard, applied successfully. Two beautiful, graceful gazelles, Adam and Steve, approached Noah but were told that only one of them could take this journey and would need a female partner. Adam and Steve complained that Noah was denying them their civil rights. Noah explained about the approaching flood and how he needed male and female of each species to procreate after the devastation that was imminent. Adam said he knew of a young, orphaned, female gazelle, who could come along to secure the future of their species when she matured. Noah said that would not work because other pairs would object to the gazelles' *ménage-a-trois*. Steve said he and Adam had every right to be considered for the cruise, as a family, and that he was going to report Noah to the Gay Rights Protective Corps.

Noah continued accepting male and female pairs of animals, excluding gazelles, as he waited to see what would happen with Adam and Steve. Having talked over the situation with Pearl, he pondered her advice to accept the trio of gazelles. In the meantime, two highly intelligent foxes applied; their names were Olivia and Justine. Noah, again, explained why they did not qualify for the trip and was threatened by them with legal action from Gay Pride Worldwide, Inc. Olivia, a down-to-earth problem solver, offered to be impregnated by Keith, their good friend, so she and Justine could contribute to the future of foxes; Justine promised to attentively care for their offspring and not let it bother the adults on board. Noah stood his ground and adhered to his original criteria for the free cruise.

In due time, Noah had heterosexual couples of all animals except for gazelles and foxes. He thought about accepting male-female pairs of gazelles and foxes but did not want to have to renege on his agreement with them, in the event that he was legally forced to accept Adam, Steve, the orphaned gazelle, Justine, and a possibly newly-impregnated Olivia.

Pearl still contended that Noah should accept the two homosexual families so they could proceed with the travel plans. Noah did not think that this was what God wanted, but he wasn't sure.

How Poor is Poor?

We all hear the term, "below the poverty level." Politicians promise to better the lot of the working class, and rescue them from being or becoming poor. Tourists who visit Haiti come home with strong visual memories of the "abject poor." Must one be homeless to be poor? Is being homeless necessarily poor? What does the word poor mean to the family of a highly paid executive (sole breadwinner) who gets laid off or fired?

Well, just how poor is poor? Is it a number on an annual gross income chart? Or is it below expectations of someday being rich? Is "poor" the same to all strata of society below the tag of middle class? Do members of the middle class ever feel poor? Or the upper class?

Poor is relative. It varies according to your expectations, to your previous standard of living, and to how your friends, relatives, and neighbors live. It also changes according to your age. Landing a great first real job in your 20's may represent to you safety from ever being poor. Some people think college education will protect them from being poor. When we are young we imagine that when we get old we will have amassed money of savings, investments, pensions, and such. However, many elderly feel poor because they know their income sources, if not meager, are limited. Poor is security-related.

A man I once knew, (single, college educated, on his way up) once said "I don't want to have to choose between a trip to Europe and private school for my (one) kid." Thus, his view of poor was very different than that of a couple struggling to feed, clothe, house, and educate their several children. His three best friends were a high-profile attorney, an orthopedic surgeon, and an heir to a meat packing business; he was a moderately successful businessman who felt poor in comparison to these three and other friends of a similar ilk. Most everyone would like to be rich or richer and no one wants to be, feel, or appear poor.

I look at males and females who stand at intersections with cardboard signs that say "Hungry. Homeless. Please Help," and I wonder how they got to that point of not having a place to live and money for food. Forget a car, designer clothes, a checkbook with a reasonable balance. Forget security, image, and ego. Just living from day to threadbare day. I would say that is poor.

We all know people of limited financial means who have a sunny outlook, a positive disposition, and contentment in their hearts. Do they know something we don't? Are they stupid for not realizing that they are money-poor? Maybe they see their riches in non-material ways. Maybe their expectations are modest. Expectations have a lot to do with what level of poorness people designate for themselves.

So let's examine some of the varied qualifications of being poor. Not being able to pay off your credit card bill every month is different from not having enough food for your family every day. Having the electricity in your house cut off for non-payment of the bill isn't the same as not taking a trip to Europe every year or putting your kids in a upscale summer camp. Dropping out of high school before graduation to get a job to bring in some money now? Putting Fido to sleep because you can't afford the vet's bill to treat him? Not attending your dad's funeral in another state because no money for plane, train or even bus fare? Giving up your car because insurance rates became prohibitive? Not having health insurance?

Yes, all of these, to some degree, equal "poor." But they are all on different levels of urgent poorness and, most important, they are all colored by the person's view of himself or herself and of poorness. A teacher I once knew, who had recently become single, told me she wanted to exhibit so much happiness that her pre-teen daughter would not realize that they were poor. And she did.

Thus, poverty and poorness are both statistical conditions and emotional interpretations.

Have you ever felt, been, or feared being poor or know anyone who did? Do you recall the trigger which preceded it?

The Business of Living

The business of living means
dealing with ghosts from the past,
preparing for the future, and
negotiating the complex super highways of the present.

Seeking an even keel between depression and euphoria.
Money: earn some, save some, spend some joyfully.
Pay the bills, but buy a few thrills.

Attempting to harmonize relationships?
Participate, support, enjoy. . . . but become not their slaves.
Cherish the healthy days and
address those that aren't, as best you can.
Don't grow obsessed or make body maintenance
a full time occupation.

Try not to let there be more month than money,
more chores than energy,
more people than patience.

Manage the budget of your requirements and
your resources so that it all comes out even.

Just live. Seek satisfaction. Pay your dues.
Hard to find that middle road and balance on it squarely.
But, try. This is the business of living.

Your Own Notes on Selections in this Book

Printed in the United States
by Baker & Taylor Publisher Services